Praise for *Not Done Yet!*

"This book spoke to me. I loved it. I have been on a journey to explore what we know about ourselves and our limitations. This has been and is my work. The book made me see that the feelings of being "powerless over my present and future" are just ideas I've told myself. As an actress, the fear of never getting another job because of my age or the way that I look stood before me for so long, and after reading this book, I see that it is important that I always advocate for myself and for other women. Thank you, Bonnie! I too am a badass woman. I can't wait to share this with other women!"

MARISSA JARET WINOKUR, Tony Award–winning actress

"*Not Done Yet!* offers a valuable road map for women over fifty. They can conquer "gendered ageism" on the job while becoming their true, best selves. Like wine, such badass women will age to perfection."

JOANN S. LUBLIN, former career columnist for *The Wall Street Journal*

"In her inimitable sassy and straight-forward way, Bonnie Marcus reminds readers that we should not and must not 'go gentle into that good night.' With humor, encouragement, and tangible tips, this book provides the impetus to take control of your life after fifty—regardless of what anyone else may have in mind for you. It's a great read!"

LOIS P. FRANKEL, PhD, author of *Nice Girls Don't Get the Corner Office* and *Ageless Women, Timeless Wisdom*

"I loved this book! I know, and my mom knew, that anything is possible at any age. I'm constantly redefining my goals and I get caught up in fear. This book helped me to see that the conflicts are between me and me. By thinking differently with optimism and hope, I can reframe my negativity into possibility and change. This book helped me see redefining my goals as a positive, and inspired me to lean into the change with badass passion."

MELISSA RIVERS, TV personality, producer, and podcaster

"Not only does Bonnie debunk myths about women's abilities after turning fifty, but she also provides tips and tools to ensure that they live the second half of their lives with courage, daring, and determination!"

LORI SOKOL, PhD, executive director, *Women's eNews*

"A powerful and very personal invitation to every woman to unleash— at last!—her inner badass in the second half of life. This book is a nudge, a guide, and a road map to stepping into our power and potential— for ourselves and for the world—after a half-century often spent serving, pleasing, and adapting."

AVIVAH WITTENBERG-COX, CEO of 20-First, gender expert, author, and TEDX speaker

"Not Done Yet! is a life-changing guide for professional women over fifty to dump limiting ideas about aging and step into their full power. With sass and attitude, Marcus lays out the challenges and opportunities of staying marketable at any age. Share it with your friends; gift it to yourself.

BONNIE ST. JOHN, Paralympic ski medalist and author of *Micro-Resilience: Minor Shifts for Major Boosts in Focus, Drive, and Energy*

"My personal motto is "mid-career at 65," so of course I'm a huge fan of *Not Done Yet!* Bonnie Marcus lays out the case for female confidence born of wisdom, experience, and the fierce desire to contribute. Her book is a guide to navigating a rich, joyous path through the second and maybe best part of working life."

SALLY HELGESEN, author of *How Women Rise, The Female Advantage* and *The Female Vision*

"As an author, podcaster, and thought leader, Bonnie Marcus is an inspiration to women everywhere, regardless of their age or career aspirations. Her new book, *Not Done Yet!,* has lessons for women who are struggling to find their direction and purpose. The timeless advice can also help younger women who may not be in touch with their badass spirits yet. I also recommend listening to her *Badass Women* podcast, which offers engaging stories from women who have overcome challenges, soared past barriers, and paved the way for new opportunities."

VERONICA VICENTE, COO, Crowe Global

"Bonnie Marcus channels her anger over ageism and her years of experience as an executive coach into a highly readable, extraordinarily helpful guide to navigating the work world after fifty. She tackles common fears that hold us back, and offers specific advice for self-advocacy and responding to ageist workplace attitudes. *Not Done Yet!* reads like a big fist in the air that will bring out the badass in all of us and remind us that getting older is a time not for apology but for pride and action."

JEANNIE RALSTON, co-founder of NextTribe

"*Not Done Yet!* encourages women to acknowledge their inner power and to execute it. This is a must-read—informative, smart, and entertaining as well. I couldn't put it down. Barbara makes crucially important truths not only about working women over fifty, but also about women who are dealing with their own feelings about aging."

BARBARA ROSE BROOKER, founder of AgeMarch.org, and author of *The Viagra Diaries* and *Love, Sometimes*

"'Assumptions, Fears, and All the Crap about Aging That Holds You Back' is my favorite chapter in this fierce book about acceptance and loving yourself. As a producer in Hollywood, I know firsthand the struggles that ageism can invite in. This book helps you see it, name it, and move towards owning your own power. Thank you, Bonnie!"

JULIE STERN, executive TV and film producer

"Bonnie Marcus is on a mission: to help older professional women fight back against ageist stereotypes. In this fast-paced book, she draws on the ups and downs of her own and her interviewees' lives to coax and cajole women to stay relevant, advocate for themselves, assertively handle ageist comments, and find fulfilment in the power of experience."

ALISON MAITLAND, co-author of *INdivisible: Radically Rethinking Inclusion for Sustainable Business Results*

"It's well documented that workplaces benefit from women in senior management, as gender-balanced teams deliver superior results. Yet women (and men) over fifty face unique challenges. In *Not Done Yet!*, Marcus takes on gendered ageism in the workplace and offers insights and practical advice challenging the status quo, office politics, and meritocracies to shove ageist assumptions out the window in order to evolve the workplace to this century."

JEFFERY TOBIAS HALTER, gender strategist and president, YWomen

"*Bonnie Marcus!* Oh, I'm not done yet! In this fabulous, irreverent, and honest book, Bonnie introduces us to the notion of declaring our power, rewriting our stories, and standing up for our position as badass women. She shares intimate glimpses into the life of a creative woman who has experienced the same fears and frustrations that lead us into deficit instead of abundance. She digs deep into her own process and shares her own stories, uniqueness, and truths, which make us feel connected to our femininity, power, and choices, as well as to ourselves and her. We are never done. I want to be her best friend!"

SUZY UNGER, MA, licensed marriage and family therapist

"Bonnie Marcus lays it all out: the fears, the self-doubt, the self-sabotage that often afflict women over fifty, and then provides direct, common sense approaches to enable her readers to find their own paths to both thriving and flourishing as they learn to savor this stage of their lives and careers."

TIMI ANYON HALLEM, partner at Manatt, Phelps & Phillips, LLP

1/15/2021

Sally,
Thank you so much for your
endorsement and support!
Bonnie

**NOT
DONE
YET!**

HOW WOMEN OVER 50 REGAIN THEIR CONFIDENCE & CLAIM WORKPLACE POWER

NOT DONE YET!

Bonnie Marcus

PAGE TWO
BOOKS

Cataloguing in publication information is
available from Library and Archives Canada.
ISBN 978-1-989603-78-9 (hardcover)
ISBN 978-1-989603-79-6 (ebook)

Some names and identifying details have been
changed to protect the privacy of individuals.

Page Two
www.pagetwo.com

Edited by Kendra Ward
Copyedited by Crissy Calhoun
Proofread by Steph VanderMeulen
Cover design by Taysia Louie
Interior design by Fiona Lee
Author photo by Madeleine Vite
Printed and bound in Canada by Friesens
Distributed in Canada by Raincoast Books
Distributed in the US and internationally by
Publishers Group West, a division of Ingram

21 22 23 24   5 4 3 2 1

www.BonnieMarcusLeadership.com

*To all the fabulous women over fifty who
have the power to change the world.*

Contents

Introduction

My rant

Okay. Right from the get-go, I'm gonna be straight with you. I'm pissed.
I consider myself to be smart, savvy, and sassy. I know I have value.
I can declare with confidence that I've evolved over the decades into
a mature, level-headed woman with extensive experience and expertise. This isn't meant to be a personal brag fest by any means, but if
it's taken that way, then let it be a brag fest for all women over fifty.
Because we all have value, and I'm pissed that society seems hell-
bent on pushing us to the sidelines and diminishing our contributions.
And I want to scream, "Hold on. Not so fast. We're NOT DONE YET!"

Not Done Yet! is a book for all working women over fifty who
are dealing with aging and the bullshit ageist assumptions and
stereotypes that keep us small. We live in a culture that worships
youthfulness and requires daily sacrifices to the beauty gods. Every
day we witness younger women in the workplace being favored. We're
also keenly aware that our skin is wrinkling, our hair is turning gray,
and that none of this is tolerated in a youth-tilted culture. We sense
our power and respect slipping away.

I see signs of my aging every time I look in the mirror. And it sucks.
Not because I'm unhappy with growing old. That's a gift! It sucks

because society won't let me and my sisters age in peace. We live in a world eager to shove women aged fifty-plus out the door to make room for younger workers. And the rationale is that anyone younger or prettier has more-value. Pure BS.

I want to feel fulfilled by my work. And I want to be respected and acknowledged for that work. I want to keep working for the foreseeable future. Like many of you, I need to keep working. Sure, I could let my hair go gray and stop using the antiaging products that minimize the visible signs of my age. But I know in my gut that I will undoubtedly face the consequences of such decisions. I fear that the more my age shows, the less respect I'll receive, the less I'll be valued in the marketplace, and that my income will suffer as a result.

Given this bias, we all have choices about what compromises we're willing to make to stay marketable and keep our jobs. Should I have an eyelift? Should I do Botox and fillers in the hopes of maintaining my status and income? But even as we take steps to erase the effects of aging, we understand deep down that aging will inevitably catch up one day. How much will it affect our careers? Navigating this is something we face as professional women over fifty.

Age-related assumptions about women go beyond the cultural bias for youth and beauty. We're told that people over fifty aren't promotable, aren't worth investing in, don't have the mental capacity or physical stamina to compete—despite evidence to the contrary. Workplace practices remain based on these ageist assumptions. Policies about hiring, firing, promotion, and compensation reveal the underlying bias. And women, unfortunately, suffer earlier because of the perceived importance of good looks and the bogus notion that aging women aren't attractive. This has a substantial impact on our career trajectories.

We accept these assumptions as the god-given truth. And the real danger is that, over time, we accept them as *our* limitations. As we internalize these beliefs, we diminish ourselves, keep ourselves small, and, as a result, accelerate our aging and jeopardize our health, job security, and financial viability. This needs to stop.

I'm pissed that years of education and solid experience cease to matter. Years of managing to balance work and raising a family, often sacrificing our well-being in the process, don't matter. *Put everyone else first.* That was the message we heard loud and clear from our mothers. Somehow, having followed that advice mitigates the guilt we feel for choosing a career, or maybe we had no choice. But we still feel guilty. We've met our bosses' demands for tight deadlines with no flexibility, no real maternity leave, and certainly no family leave. Yeah, we've done all this. We may even have additional caregiving responsibilities for our parents just as we're experiencing an empty nest. Whew. When does it end?

Now, here come the fifties. Menopause, hot flashes, raging hormones, and we still go to work each day trying to do our best to win approval, acknowledgment, and promotions. But we sense change on the horizon. Our once sought-after opinion is dismissed, our workload reassigned. Younger people are promoted around us as we're pushed into the shadows of irrelevance. Demeaning remarks about older people create an environment of fear, especially for those of us who feel the pressure to remain youthfully attractive to stay employed. We ask ourselves, *What's going to happen to me? Will I be forced out? And if that happens, who will hire me?* The fear is palpable for those of us sensitive to the changing tide.

Yet I'm here to tell you, if we approach our fifties, sixties, and beyond without that awareness, we may be blindsided, believing our track record will allow us to prevail until retirement, believing that we'll be treated with dignity and respect because of our past success. We need to wake up. That isn't reality! We need to deal with our own *mishegas*, our own craziness about aging, create a strong positive image for ourselves, and march on boldly. We need to adopt a badass, winning attitude and do it ASAP—before we fall victim to continued age and gender discrimination. We need to regain our confidence and power to claim our rightful place in the world. The world desperately needs our wisdom, our experience, our voices more than ever.

There's absolutely no point crying over lost youth, expending a ton of energy wishing you were thirty again, wishing you looked more youthful. Right now, at this point in your career, you have what it takes to continue to thrive. You need to celebrate who you are, what you've achieved, and what potential you still have to make a difference. Because despite all this ageist bullshit, lots of positives and opportunities are out there for you. Reject the belief that it's all downhill from here. Turn all this around and take back control of your life and career. That's why I wrote this book. It's time for women fifty and beyond to claim their workplace power. You can do it. We can do it. We're *Not Done Yet!* And in this book, I give you the tools to step up and own your talent and the power of your age.

The solution

The first thing to do is to ditch all the fears and assumptions that keep you small, that prevent you from living your life to the fullest and thriving in your career. Part One of this book, "Assumptions, Fears, and All the Crap about Aging That Holds You Back," is a guide for you to recognize what beliefs about aging you are currently holding on to that don't serve you. There are coaching exercises in this section and throughout the book, so use a notebook or journal to record your responses to the exercises, along with any insights and emotions that surface as you do so.

Part Two, "Stop Playing Small, and Do What It Takes to Stay in the Game," offers you the tools you need to stay marketable and keep your job. Yes, I know that what you experience every day as an older woman in the workplace brings you down. It's the double whammy of gendered ageism. You need to consciously decide to fight for what you deserve, maintain your status, and continue to succeed, if not for your financial security, then for your self-esteem. These chapters give you specific guidance on how to step up your game at work and create the visibility and credibility you need, despite the prevalence of bias. It's more important than ever before to understand and communicate your value, speak up, and pull yourself out of the shadows. I'll guide you through this.

The last part, "Be Your Badass Self," helps you regain your confidence and power by adopting a badass attitude. Maybe you were a badass little girl or maybe you've always been the compliant good girl. (I confess I transitioned from a badass little girl to a compliant good girl as I grew up.) Whether a badass mindset is familiar or foreign to you, you need it now to face the adverse circumstances you face at work and in life because of your age. And by "badass," I don't mean an angry, chip-on-her-shoulder woman. "Badass" doesn't mean "bitch." Being a badass means owning who you are, owning your experience, your wisdom, your talent, your age. A badass mindset gives you swagger, and you need this now, girlfriend. Perhaps you've always needed more confidence, but now's the time to act. Now you may be challenged like never before at work and you need to fight back. You may be held hostage by ageist assumptions and now is *not* the time to escape by cowering in the background, hoping no one will take notice of your age. Quite the opposite. You need to confront your situation head-on. The fight I'm talking about means taking back control, losing the doormat mentality, putting yourself front and center, and standing up for yourself.

I'm not suggesting an external makeover for a youthful look, although that's an option if you want it. I'm talking about an internal makeover that boosts your confidence and energy. I'm talking about using your badass energy to do your best work and get the recognition you deserve, not a pink slip. I'm talking about adopting new skills and improving those you already have, practicing self-care, and writing a new, powerful story for yourself, for now and the rest of your life. That makeover starts immediately.

Say it out loud: "*I'm not done yet!*" Own it. Live it. Your livelihood and well-being depend on you believing in your value and your future. So, put on your big-girl panties and step up.

Are you with me?

Part One

ASSUMPTIONS, FEARS, AND ALL THE CRAP ABOUT AGING THAT HOLDS YOU BACK

Most of my life I've been pretty clueless about how my fears and assumptions have stifled me. I never really gave it too much thought until I started coaching other women to overcome their self-imposed barriers. Now with an increased attention to it, I've become much more aware of how my own bullshit has hindered my success and restricted my ability to experience joy. I work every day to push aside the beliefs that don't serve me. But I have to say this: managing negative thoughts and emotions isn't easy and it's an ongoing battle for all of us.

In reality, we're all held prisoner by our beliefs. However, if these beliefs happen to be positive, we can count on them for support and encouragement when we need them. They can be our rock. One such belief might be that things will always turn out okay in the end. That belief gives you the confidence that no matter how difficult your current situation, there will be a light at the end of the tunnel. This allows you to plow through some terrible times with the optimism that there are better circumstances on the horizon.

The negative voices in your head have an opposite effect. I'm sure you hear the same voices many of us hear. *I'm not smart enough, not pretty enough. I'll never be successful. I'm afraid people won't like me if they really know me. I'm afraid my ideas aren't worth sharing. My colleagues will laugh at my ideas and ridicule me.* Any of this sound familiar? Negative voices keep you from fully showing up at work and owning your talent and authenticity. This chatter goes on for most of our lives. But that inner monologue morphs over time to include a lot of limiting beliefs and fears about aging, and that's where we are now.

I'm telling you straight out: the fears and assumptions you have about aging will dramatically affect your ability to stay marketable and employed. No BS. And so, in this part, I call your attention to some of the ageist beliefs you may have that perhaps you're unaware of, because these have tremendous potential to sabotage your ongoing success and well-being. Once you have a better understanding of what they are and their influence, you can work to reframe the negative to support a more positive mindset. That positivity is essential in order for you to build your confidence to take on workplace challenges. You need an all-hands-on-deck approach to maintain your career as you age.

I don't promise that I've covered every fear and assumption about being a fifty-plus professional woman. But as you read this section and do the exercises, you will have the opportunity to investigate your own personal beliefs, the ones that don't serve you and that set you up for failure. If you have positive assumptions, by all means, amplify them! But let's work on pushing the BS out of our lives as much as possible. This you control. And controlling your mindset is one of the most powerful badass things you can do. So, let's do it.

I'm Too Old
to Get Promoted

I WAS FORTY-NINE YEARS old when I lost out on a promotion despite the fact that I'd worked my butt off, given my life to that company for nearly a decade, and had a consistent record of great performance. The rejection sucked. I felt betrayed and I was pissed. Instead of the VP job I wanted, they offered me a lateral position of AVP that would require me to relocate, which I took as another slap in the face. So, I left the company. Sayonara. Did I mention they gave the VP job to a man?

I was almost fifty and looking for a job. That wasn't something I had planned for by any means. I had naively thought I had some kind of job security because I was a top performer. I also believed, perhaps also naively, that although it might take some time, it wouldn't be difficult to find another position in a new company. That actually worked out to be true for me. I reached out to my network of former colleagues and let them know I was on the lookout for another job, and my dear friend Cheryl told me about an opening for a CEO position in her organization. I interviewed and got the job. It was a big promotion.

I could have let the experience of being passed over teach me that I was too old to get promoted. Yet never once did I think that I wouldn't land a higher-level job just because I had reached the big five-O. That belief would have sabotaged me. I wouldn't have been able to confidently position myself. Never once did I believe that I wasn't marketable. I believed the opposite was true. I was just coming off an incredible eight years at my last company. I grew my region from $10 million to $150 million. I opened new offices, expanded services, and won every award the company had to offer. So, yeah, I knew I was marketable despite losing out on the VP job I wanted. I was optimistic about my future.

Here's my point: at this age, you're at the peak of your career. This is when you have the most to offer. You know more today than you've ever known. So, if you're looking for a promotion, ask yourself this: Why should your age limit your value? You now have more experience and wisdom than ever before. Age enhances your value.

Experience = value

Wisdom = value

Therefore, age = value

See what I mean?

Listen, you didn't get to where you are today by slacking off. You didn't put in long hours and juggle work-life responsibilities or do the political dance at work for nothing. You've worked hard. You've accomplished a lot over the course of your career so far. And guess what? You're not done yet, so stop telling yourself you are!

Does your track record suddenly have no value? That's bullshit. You deserve to be promoted.

Look at the some of the world's most powerful women who were promoted after fifty. At the age of sixty, Ruth Bader Ginsburg was appointed to the Supreme Court by President Clinton, and she remained there until her death, at eighty-seven. Nancy Pelosi was sixty-seven when she first became Speaker of the House, and then again at seventy-nine. And if you look at the top-ranked women CEOs of Fortune 500 companies, nine of the top ten are over fifty and the only woman who isn't fifty is forty-nine as of this writing.

Did any of these women think they were too old to get promoted? Can you imagine Nancy Pelosi saying, "I'm grateful to you for honoring me with this position of Speaker of the House, but I think I'm too old to accept it"? How would that go? All of these women put themselves out there to get promoted. They wanted it. They're ambitious and they don't believe that ambition has a timetable. They know their value. And by the way, consider the consequences for us if they weren't in these positions!

I often tell my clients that they're stingy if they hold themselves back and don't push themselves out of their comfort zone to do what it takes to get promoted. They're stingy because they have so much value to offer their team, their manager, their company. Sure, a promotion benefits you personally. You get more responsibility and power, more recognition, and probably more money. But your promotion also benefits others who will reap the rewards of your leadership and wisdom.

Don't let your chronological age be the barrier to your ongoing success.

But let's say you *do* believe you're too old to be promoted. Follow me on this. How does this belief hold you back?

Here's an example. If Barb believes she won't get promoted because of her age, it decreases her motivation and energy level at work. She feels like a victim and, consequently, powerless to control her future. She no longer volunteers for highly visible assignments, which takes her off the radar. She rarely offers her opinions, which decreases her credibility. She simply does the work required and nothing more. She most likely appears tired and disinterested in what's going on around her. She doesn't engage. She feels like an outsider at work, isolated and uncomfortable.

So, her belief becomes a self-fulfilling prophecy. She will not get the promotion, but it may not be because of her age. It may be because she has unconsciously taken herself out of the competition.

Light bulb!

There is a direct link between your assumptions and your attitude and behavior at work, which can set you up to be marginalized without your being aware of it.

Let's reframe this and create a positive mantra to replace the negative belief that you are too old to be promoted:

I'm smart and ambitious, and I have a lot of value to offer my organization going forward.

Doesn't that feel better? Why tell yourself your days of career advancement are over? Don't let yourself get distracted by this bullshit.

Write out your own positive mantra, keep it visible, and say it out loud each day.

Instead of thinking about all the reasons you won't be promoted, start a list of all the reasons you deserve to be promoted.

It might look like this:

- I introduce innovative ideas that keep our customers engaged and loyal.

- My work has resulted in $_____ of revenue in the past year.

- I have strong relationships with our clients, who trust me to handle their most challenging issues.

- I help our team see the customer's perspective, which builds strong relationships.

- Over the course of my career, I've learned how to wisely assess situations and find strategic solutions.

- My value only increases with age as I bring to my team the many lessons I've learned about business over the years.

- Individuals across the company respect me, trust me, and look to me for advice and leadership.

- I'm ready, willing, and able for this promotion.

Create your own list of at least three to five reasons you should get promoted, and focus on them going forward.

Here's my point: as soon as you believe you're too old, you'll be stuck where you are for the remainder of your career, and you'll sabotage your future success. Is that really what you want? Don't be afraid. Forget the self-doubt. This is your life and your career. Go for what you want and deserve.

I'm Too Old to Compete

I GET A LITTLE weary of all the fuss made about young people in the workplace. *How can we appeal to younger generations? What's important to them?* Companies are bending over backwards, sideways, and every which way to make their workplaces more appealing to employees under thirty. That's fine, but what about the rest of us? There are six generations in the workforce today, and we all have a lot to offer and deserve respect.

We witness the bias in favor of younger workers. They're considered smarter and better suited to get ahead. We see this playing out every day, and then we're suckered into believing it ourselves. We believe we're too old to compete. What happens when we believe this? We accept it as the truth and voluntarily step out of the spotlight and keep ourselves small. We believe that we don't have what it takes to compete, therefore we *don't* compete. We perpetuate the myth by not throwing our hat in the ring for top jobs and thwart our future advancement in the process. We unconsciously remove ourselves from competing or we consciously talk ourselves out of even trying.

Do you see what's happening here? The workplace reflects society's bias against older workers and this leads companies to make ageist decisions about hiring, firing, and compensation. But instead of staking our claim and believing in our value and our continued contribution, we also come to believe we're too old, and that's just crap. I don't care how old you are—fifty, sixty, or seventy. Your value doesn't diminish with each birthday. It increases in many ways.

Do you hold back from competing for fear you'll be called out as too old, for fear people will laugh at you? Trust me: if you're just biding your time in your job until retirement and not actively contributing new ideas and opinions, people will likely notice and justifiably label you as a dead weight, a dinosaur. And, let's face it, if you're just coasting along in your job without actively contributing, you're acting like one. You're setting yourself up for extinction by not keeping yourself in the game.

Christie Ciraulo and her team of Mighty Mermaids, all women over sixty, swam across the English Channel in 2019. Did they think of themselves as too old to compete? Not for a minute. They trained with focus and determination every day in the pool or out in the open water. They knew exactly what they needed to do to reach their goal, and they weren't afraid to pursue it. No excuses like *I'm too old*. They're probably more physically fit at sixty than most thirty-year-olds. What's important is that they have an all-in attitude. That's what it takes to compete. You set the goal and go after it, despite the obstacles. You don't take an I'll-dip-one-little-toe-in-to-test-the-water-and-see-how-it-goes approach.

I suck at most sports, but I recognize that I don't necessarily lack the skill, I'm just not a competitor in this arena. As a result, I hesitate and hold myself back. I don't seem to have the killer instinct to beat my opponent at tennis or golf, and it costs me match after match. I know what it feels like to hold yourself back from competing. Yes, in a way, it's a cop-out. I'll tell you why.

I had a phone conversation not long ago with a guy in his thirties who was fired from his job after just a couple of years. He's been unsure of what he wants in his career and has jumped around a bit. He confessed that he has never quite felt that he fit in a role and has held himself back from engaging 100 percent in any of his jobs. I pointed out to him that not going all in with his job was his protection. He can always look back and say, *Well, I never gave it my all, so it's not really my failure.* By not competing, he plays it safe. Are you doing the same thing? What's that going to cost you?

By the way, I mentioned killer instinct in relation to being competitive and winning. That "killer instinct" label gives competition a bad rap. Competing isn't a bad thing. It doesn't necessarily mean stepping over others to reach your goal, if that notion holds you back from competing. I'm not a great competitor on the tennis court or golf course, but I am competitive. I compete with myself every day. When I go for a run, I compete with myself. How long did it take me to complete my run? Did I increase my distance? I'm always trying to be better at whatever I do, and that mindset of always improving is critical for you at this point in your career. The only danger here is being hypercritical; don't beat yourself up by setting the bar way too high. Yeah, I catch myself doing that a lot and I always need to remind myself to manage my expectations and not lose sight of reality.

Show up and be the best you can be. Competing is all about staying in the game, not withdrawing because you think you're too old or lacking in skills. If your skills need an update, do it. A friend of mine was recently laid off: her organization said that she didn't have the technical skills to manage online learning, which was necessary for her role going forward. Be proactive and stay on top of the skills you need. Don't hold yourself back. Do what it takes to compete in the workplace and remain marketable.

Here's the thing: if you don't truly go for it, you'll never know what can happen if you really try, if you wholeheartedly compete, and that's a pity. If you're holding back now and not fully engaged with your work, you may be protecting yourself but also setting yourself up for failure. Keep in mind that as an older woman in the workplace today, your performance is under a microscope. There's no denying that forces out there would love to cut you out of their budget and reduce costs, and you're fair game. You need to remain competitive to survive.

Remember Helen Reddy's song "I Am Woman"? That was the empowerment song of women in the Boomer generation. Not too long ago, I experienced the song performed at a live concert, and the band welcomed all women in the audience to the stage to sing and dance. It was a joyous celebration of feminine power to be on that stage with women of all ages who were so connected to the lyrics that declare our determination that we women can do anything. We can't allow ourselves to lose that sense of power, collectively or individually. Don't let go of that commitment to reach your goal.

Personally (sports aside), I'm an all-in kind of gal. All in for me means putting my heart and soul into something and not worrying about the outcome from the get-go. I follow my heart in relationships as well as my work. Sometimes that makes me a bit impulsive and I get burned, but for the most part I'm strategic and weigh the pros and cons of a situation and think through what it means to jump in and compete.

I didn't even start my business career until I was thirty-five. Newly divorced with two young children, I had been a kindergarten teacher and aerobics instructor, and neither of those professions paid the bills. So, I threw myself into the big-business world with absolutely no business training or experience, and I went from an entry-level position to CEO of a national company in fifteen years. I needed to be successful. When that CEO gig ended, I reinvented myself and did some consulting work, which landed me a great job as VP of sales for a tech start-up, then another job as VP of sales at fifty-two. I started my own business at fifty-nine, and I've never looked back. I never doubted my willingness to compete.

Are you aware that Julia Child didn't start her cooking career until she was in her forties? She was inspired after eating a delicious meal of sole meunière in France. That mind-blowing experience inspired her to take cooking lessons and spend countless hours learning how to cook and bake, and from there her business empire began. She didn't let her age stop her from following her passion and building her career. Can you imagine what would have happened if she had? I, for one, would never know how to make coq au vin or boeuf bourguignonne with her special flare.

Grandma Moses didn't start painting until she was in her eighties. Laura Ingalls Wilder didn't publish *Little House on the Prairie* until she was sixty-five. Did these women let their age hold them back? No way!

What's your career goal at this point in your life? Is it to fade into the woodwork or is it to continue to thrive? If your financial future is at stake, you don't have a choice, sister, but to jump in and compete. Don't do it halfheartedly or you will fail. Challenge yourself and give your career your full energy and focus. Make it your mission to finish your career on your terms with a bang, not a whimper. You'll never know how powerful and successful you can be unless you try.

I'm No Longer Attractive

I LOVE IT WHEN someone tells me I look young. I graciously accept what I believe is meant to be a compliment. Of course, let's face it, what they leave out is "for your age," because although I admit I look pretty damn good "for my age," I certainly don't look young anymore.

Looks are important to me. Appearance matters a lot. I absorbed subtle messages that appearance matters from my mother, who was so drop-dead gorgeous that people still talk about her beauty years after her passing. It mattered a lot to my mom, who never went a day without lipstick and had her hair done weekly until her mid-nineties when she died. So, yes, I also pay a great deal of attention to how I look. Not sure if it's genetic or environmental, but it is what it is.

If I'm having a bad hair day, it can affect how I show up in the world. Some days I say to hell with it, I'm just too tired to wash, blow dry, and flat iron my hair. Yet I finally have admitted to myself that I feel better when I look good. It sounds a bit shallow to say that, but it's true. I wear a little makeup every day even though I work from home and the only one who sees me most days is the checkout person at Trader Joe's. My point is that I want to feel attractive and believe (with a little help from makeup) that I still can be attractive *for my age.*

As I get older, I struggle with empowerment versus vanity. Go gray? No way. Of course, dyeing your hair gray is considered hip in your twenties and thirties, but that's before the wrinkles show up. The combination of gray hair and a mature face is a whole different ball game. All the twenty-year-olds who dye their hair gray aren't making a statement about how wonderful it is to be old. Likely they are saying the opposite: *Look at me, I can have gray hair and still look young and beautiful.*

I had dinner with a couple of my girlfriends recently. They both get Botox and fillers, and they asked me point-blank, "Why look old and tired when you can do something about it?" Were they implying I looked old and tired? As soon as I got home, I checked myself out in the mirror. *Mirror, mirror on the wall* . . . doesn't lie. In comparison to their radiant faces, I do look old and tired. I do have bags under my eyes, crow's feet, and all the visible signs that I'm no longer the fresh young ingenue I once was. You know, if our society didn't applaud youth and beauty to the extent that it does, likely none of us would feel so insecure about aging. I'm fairly certain this sensitivity is not in our DNA, but I could be wrong about that. Absent the pressure to appear perpetually thirty, I can imagine myself gazing in the mirror and feeling pretty satisfied with how I look for the rest of my life.

But it's hard to escape the strong, ever-present message that women need to look youthful and attractive to get anywhere in life. Research confirms that attractiveness positively affects income. No doubt, over the course of your career, you've noticed that good-looking women have an advantage. Frankly, this causes my blood to boil because it reeks of unfairness and because a naive part of me would love to believe that looks don't matter. But, every day at work, we witness that they do. Attractive people get hired and promoted faster, and this message rings loud and clear.

As you age and feel this pressure, and witness the privileged treatment of younger, pretty women in the workplace, you may unconsciously retreat. And every time you pull back, you marginalize yourself and confirm assumptions that you have less value, energy, and ambition. Your self-consciousness and insecurity about your looks affect your willingness to advocate for yourself, to raise your hand and speak up, to volunteer for highly visible projects—all of which are essential for staying in the game.

At the beginning of this chapter, I confessed that having a bad hair day affects my confidence and my mood. Believing that you're no longer attractive is like having a bad hair day *every day*. Recognize that, at this stage of your career especially, this limiting belief detracts from your ongoing success because it leads you to avoid doing what you need to do to remain competitive.

Of course, millions of women all over the world believe they're no longer attractive once that first wrinkle appears. There's a whole empire built on the demand for women to look young and pretty. The global antiaging market is predicted to reach $292.5 billion by 2025, and in 2017 alone, over $16 billion was spent in the US on cosmetic surgery, all because of our fear of looking old and tired.

And there's no question about it. I somewhat buy into the hype. I spend $165 on a jar of antiaging cream, which I wouldn't want to give up, even if it meant not eating for a week. There's something about the subtle smell of lavender and the creamy texture that feels like an indulgence with every application. Honestly, I have no idea if it works, but I'm addicted. I also get facials every month. The facials are marketed as antiaging, with various serums and creams designed to work miracles and turn back the clock. They don't really turn back the clock. My skin glows for an hour after the treatment and then I'm back to normal. However, truth be told, facials are good for you. They exfoliate, getting rid of dead cells and dirt that clog up your pores, and hydrate the skin, which is much needed as we age. They also make me feel like I'm being proactive and doing something to delay the inevitable signs of aging.

Actors are our role models, for better or worse, when it comes to our appearance. How can you help but compare yourself with women your age who are in public view? Many of them look great—with a lot of help—and it distorts our idea of what an aging woman should look like. Yet, in my opinion, many have had way too many interventions. I was shocked when I saw the new versions of Meg Ryan, Renée Zellweger, and Cher, who's timeless but plastic. Dolly Parton takes an empowered approach by admitting she has had surgeries and is proud of how she looks. But too much Botox and you look like a zombie. Too much filler and you look like Howdy Doody. (Oops, I'm dating myself.)

I have a newly acquired fascination with all this. I find it an interesting pastime to identify whether women I see in film, on TV, or in everyday life have had work done. Possibly it's part of my own evaluation process about whether I'll do something in the future. Who knows? But it's hard to tell these days what's natural and what isn't, unless it's done in excess. During a recent trip to Paris, I was sitting in a café next to a couple having lunch. The woman caught my attention. I guessed that she was in her seventies at least, but her face didn't have one wrinkle. Her skin was smooth and shiny. Her lips were big, a little too big, and full. But you know what? She still looked old. What gave her age away? Her neck, her arms, her hands. So, sometimes I'm not sure what we have to gain from all this stuff. I mean, come on, we can't redo our whole body. Or can we? Or do we even want to?

How should we handle the issue of feeling we're no longer attractive as we age? We can make fun of ourselves like Nora Ephron, who dedicated an entire book to her aging, sagging neck. Her neck obsession is hilarious and I found myself laughing out loud reading the book. But it also made me a bit sad and then mad, because society shows so much disdain for older women. Why shouldn't we be considered attractive at fifty, sixty, seventy, and beyond? And why don't we feel attractive as we age? When did wrinkles become shameful and when did we start buying into all this bullshit? Doesn't it piss you off?

It pisses me off even though I buy into it! When do we accept the fact that we look good just the way we are?

I'm not going to tell you how you should feel about your appearance. As women, we never seem to be satisfied with our looks, *ever*, even when we're young. I remember being self-conscious about my curly, frizzy hair when I was a little girl. In my preteens, I went through a chubby stage and I wasn't exactly cover girl material. Add braces to that picture and I looked like an alien. Thank god the braces worked (although I didn't wear my retainer and then had to foot the bill myself for braces a second time as an adult—now I wear that damn thing to bed every night), and I thank the hair goddesses that keratin relaxers work. For a few years in high school and college, I ironed my hair. Right on the ironing board. Yup. Ever smelled burnt hair? It's god-awful.

There was a window of time from my thirties to about fifty when my evil inner critic was fairly happy with how I looked. My point is that this focus on looking attractive is not new. It's just different now. When I was thirteen, I was concerned my boobs weren't big enough. All the girls in my class were already wearing bras, and although my chest had barely developed, I convinced my mom that I desperately needed one and wore white shirts to let everyone know I had finally made it through that rite of passage. Now things are sagging, wrinkling, and drooping and we're constantly bombarded with messages that this is bad. We're taunted by magazine covers of teenage girls masquerading as adults and actors who've had lots of cosmetic interventions. It's alarming and confusing. What are we supposed to look like as we age?

I'd like to tell you to rise above it all and focus on your inner qualities that are unique and magnetic. You know, deep down, it's those qualities that matter, or at least they should.

Bottom line: it's your choice here. You can fight to look younger than you are for the rest of your life, or you can learn to love and accept yourself and be grateful for being on this planet another day, wrinkles and all. Honestly, most days I fall somewhere in between these two sentiments. Looking good makes me feel more confident, which helps my career and my relationships and my attitude.

Whatever path you choose, from acceptance to aggressive interventions, I hope you know that people love and respect you for who you are. And whatever approach you take to aging, there's no judgment. In the workplace, lead with your talent and experience. Don't give credence to the bullshit assumptions about aging. Be aware that your own beliefs about this could harm your career. Show up as professional and powerful. In your life, find a path that works for you and own it.

I Need to Look Young to Succeed

OKAY, NOW I'm not talking about vanity. I'm talking about the really serious stuff: your ability to keep your job, and the fragility of your financial future and security based on your appearance. If you're feeling some anxiety about your future as you begin to show visible signs of aging, I'm with you on this. The whole notion that your looks can influence your success may be real, but your belief that the *only* way you'll continue to thrive in your career is if you look young is bullshit. Buying into that assumption is going to derail you for sure.

Women I interviewed for this book commented on all the fuss made about attractive young women in the workplace. Yeah, they seem to get all the attention. Men gravitate to them, engage them in conversation, sit next to them at meetings, truly enjoy being in their presence. And here's my true confession. When I was a pretty young thing, I took every advantage of that attention to build relationships and influence. I'm not implying I slept my way to the top, because I never compromised myself that way, but I recognized that senior leadership, all male, thought I was attractive and enjoyed spending time with me. I used that time and attention to my advantage to get more high-profile assignments and opportunities. I leveraged the attention to build the credibility I needed. There's no doubt: a woman's looks are important in the workplace.

Lois Frankel, a well-known and respected coach and author, shared with me her experience interviewing at one of the large studios in Hollywood a few years ago. The top executive was looking for a coach.

> They brought me in to meet with her. I had just gotten over chemo-therapy. So, my hair was just starting to grow back. It was growing back white. Not even gray, just kind of a pure white. And I sat down and I met with her. I was in my fifties at the time. And I thought the meeting went really well. And obviously I have a lot of coaching experience. But I didn't get selected to coach her. So, I contacted the HR person and I said, "If I could just get any feedback. If I did some-thing wrong, I'd certainly want to know so I wouldn't do it again." And the only thing she said to me was "Lois, ours is a youth culture."

What does that mean? The fact that Lois showed up with white hair most likely cost her the job.

Lois said that, in her opinion, women need to stay competitive: "After I got that feedback, 'This is a youth culture,' I dyed my hair again. I was going to let it stay white and I guess if I was simply a feminist, I'd say, 'Well, nobody's going to dictate to me how I should look.' Well, wait a minute. What I want is work and I want to be considered rele-vant. And I want to be listened to. And if that's the case and that takes dyeing my hair blond again, so be it."

Lois's point is a good one. We need to do what it takes to keep working. But whether or not to enhance or modify your looks to stay employed or get hired depends on the work environment and your personal feelings. Take Lois's experience interviewing in a Holly-wood studio. Hollywood is extremely focused on youth and beauty, maybe more so than other work environments. Lois received feedback about a youth culture and dyed her hair to prevent age from factoring against her getting work in the future. Covering your gray might help an employer focus more on your talent than your age. But changing your hair won't always cut it. Most companies are looking for talent and for a cultural fit, and even with blond hair, no one over fifty looks thirty. That's the damn truth.

Lois went on to illustrate her point.

Look at Jane Fonda. Look at what she has done to remain relevant. And is that vain? I don't think it's vain. I think she wants to keep working. And so, it may take a face-lift or a tummy tuck or whatever for her to do that. In one of my books I said, and this is directed at younger people, "If something about yourself makes you lack self-confidence, then have it cut, colored, tucked, lifted, snipped, whatever it takes to give you confidence." And there's nothing wrong with that. And again, according to your values. I'm not saying that it's right for everybody, but for some people.

Sharon was recently laid off from an architectural interior design company.

Women are not allowed to look old in commercial real estate, in interior design, in the architectural realm. You're expected to continue to have a very polished and young appearance on the external client side, especially if you're doing business development and you're bringing in work. And so a week and a half ago, I had eye lift surgery. If I had not been laid off, would I have done that? No... But if I want to work for the next ten years, as far as I'm concerned, this is an investment in my future job. And so if you'd asked me before, "Is that something you would do?" I would've said, "Why would I need to do that?" I'm not doing it because I'm vain. I'm doing it because this investment in money and time could help me work for another ten years. And so for me it was a very practical decision. And I just wonder about the other women in the marketplace. I know all the female realtors, the commercial brokers in the architectural industry, all those women kind of age out of the industry... Their client base starts to decline. And the ones that refresh their appearance... hang in that industry longer. And just observing that and seeing that in the industry, it was something I knew at some point I would have to face, and it's just something you deal with.

Something we have to deal with? This causes my blood to boil, but Lois and Sharon are right in their assessment of the situation. Research confirms that we face age discrimination earlier than men because of the importance placed on our looks. I hate, hate, hate this. And here's the killer: we're perceived to be less competent as we show signs of aging. Plain and simple, this type of judgment, based on our appearance, affects our livelihood. It dramatically tips the already unlevel playing field in favor of men.

So, here we are. We're fifty and beyond. We've worked hard and achieved a lot and now we have to face the reality that our wrinkles and gray hair affect our future. As Lois Frankel said, "If you choose to enhance your appearance to keep your job, that's your decision." I agree. There's no judgment here. I believe the women who've shared their stories with me sincerely felt their success depended on maintaining a youthful appearance. They made an empowered decision.

You need to do what is right for you, even as we all admit this biased pressure sucks. You may say to yourself, *I'm not compromising who I am for anyone. I'm owning my age and not apologizing for it. I'm proud of my wrinkles. I've earned every one of them. I love my gray hair. So, I'm going focus more on what it takes to stay marketable by improving my skills and advocating for myself and my work.* Or you may choose to enhance your appearance and overall well-being with non-invasive techniques such as dyeing your hair, good skincare, and attention to your makeup and wardrobe along with doing what it takes to stay in the game. Or you can opt to do it all. The bottom line is that gendered ageism is a factor in our careers. There's no denying it. How you respond is your personal decision based on your values and perhaps the culture of your workplace.

However, you can't hide behind the assumption that looking young is the only factor that affects your career. Modifying your appearance alone doesn't ensure your success. It may help you show up more confidently, which is important, but if you believe you can succeed only if you look young, you'll focus solely on your external appearance and not on the internal traits: your strengths, your talent, your history, and your wisdom. The stuff that gets results. You can't point to aging as an excuse for not doing the work you need to do to continue to be a valuable and viable force in the workplace.

I've already confessed that my looks are important to me, and I believe they're important to some degree for my career. I don't try to look super-young, which would be fruitless at this point without surgery, but I don't want to look frumpy either. Like you, I want and need to work. I want to continue to coach and speak. Looking younger probably doesn't hurt, but it isn't as critical for my ongoing success as my background and talent are. I doubt anyone decides to hire me as their coach based on my looks.

Here's the thing: Would you really want to turn back the clock? I wouldn't. Seriously, you'd be twenty or thirty years younger, but you wouldn't be who you are today. It's the whole package that counts. What's marketable is your wisdom and talent. I know right now you're probably saying to yourself, *That's crap, Bonnie*. But again, you have a choice here. You can mope around the office feeling like the cards are stacked against you, act out with anger, and let everyone see the major chip on your shoulder. Or you can become a recluse hiding in the shadows. Let me tell you, girlfriend, neither of these mindsets is going to help you succeed.

Own your bullshit. Listen to your harsh inner critic's message about how you're not going to succeed because you no longer look young and tell her to take a hike. Give your inner critic a name. I call mine Gertrude, actually Trudy, because we're close in a toxic, codependent kind of way. But I often tell Trudy, *Shut the f**k up, go to hell, you're interfering with my life.* What do you want to say to your inner critic when she tells you that you won't succeed because you don't look young? Spare the niceties. It works. Mind you, she's never going to completely disappear, but your best path forward is to give her less attention, no matter how hard she tries to get it.

And stop comparing your looks to thirty-year-olds'. Where does that get you? It's a rabbit hole you don't want to fall into. It's going to lead you to a dark place without an exit. They look great, sure. But you have a boatload more experience, wisdom, and savvy. They have decades of missteps yet to endure, the ones you've already learned lessons from (some of which may have added a wrinkle or two). Be proud of who you are today, your journey, your talent. And be proud of how you look. But most importantly, be proud of how you show up every day, feeling comfortable in your own skin, being your magnificent you. Who you are today is the sum total of everything: your smarts, experience, temperament, personality, and yes, your appearance. Own your whole package. Celebrate it. It's the only package you'll ever have.

I'm Irrelevant

O F ALL THE ageist assumptions we may believe about ourselves, this one really gets to me. It's not that it pisses me off as do some of the other assumptions we hold. It's that it makes me terribly sad. Why would anyone believe that she's irrelevant? Feeling that you're irrelevant is like feeling you have nothing to offer, like no one cares what you think or feel. You're marginalized, pushed aside, a shadow of your former self. If you believe this, you're in dangerous territory. Taking on this assumption challenges your very existence as a human being, as a woman. No one alive today is irrelevant. I don't care who you are or what you do: you matter.

But I get it. I honestly do. I've heard from enough women whose opinions are routinely dismissed, whose workload is redistributed to younger colleagues, who aren't invited to important meetings, who are basically ignored at work. Naturally, they begin to believe they're irrelevant. That's the way they're being treated.

But I need to remind you that on a basic level, if you're breathing today, you're relevant. No joke. I don't care what the assholes at work are doing to you. We all have the right to be alive and to pursue a career and thrive. And like I've said before, if you hold ageist beliefs, you're giving away your power and perpetuating stereotypes about the value of older women in the workplace. It's your responsibility to call yourself out on this stuff and catch yourself acting as if all this BS is true. Challenge yourself to recognize your sabotaging beliefs and subsequent behavior. Your thoughts and actions are the only things you can control.

Kate shared with me that she would tell herself to *just keep going.*

Don't let them get to you. I made a point of trying not to be invisible, to make it easy for people to have me work for them. In other words, I began to think and understand that, *you know what? It's my role to make me an employee that they value.* Even if they don't see it, I can make that happen. I'll be the one that raises the question. I'll be the one that goes over and says, "Hey how about this?" I'll be the one that moves my chair into the huddles that I'm excluded from even when the topic's relevant to me. I'll be the icebreaker. It's up to me because no one's going to come over here and talk to me... I didn't wait for someone to say, "What's your opinion?" I made sure I offered it.

I love Kate's attitude. What's *your* plan to demonstrate your relevance? Jot down some motivational ideas about how you intend to show everyone how you are relevant. Here are a few ideas:

- I'll be the one who steps up to volunteer for projects that matter to key stakeholders.

- I'll be the one who supports and encourages my team to do their best work.

- I'll be a mentor and motivator for my younger colleagues.

- I'll share my ideas to solve problems and improve productivity and efficiency with my team and manager.

- I'll suggest social events that everyone can feel comfortable participating in.

You are relevant. You matter. You have opinions and ideas. You have skills and great experience. You have a commitment to your work. You're curious. You're smart. You have tons of value to contribute. Are you relevant? You bet.

I'm Powerless over
My Present and Future

OKAY. LISTEN UP, because this is important. If you believe
that you no longer have power because you're a fifty-year-old
woman, then you need to recognize that you're either consciously or unconsciously giving it up. The power is still there within
you. But you're unplugging yourself from the source.

Here's the thing about power: no one can give it to you. Even when
you have a big title and people assume that you have power, if you
don't own it, soon everyone will see through the facade. And you'll
feel it too. You'll wake up one day and think, *What the hell happened?
I'm a VP of this company and I can't get anything done.* But take note:
no one can truly take your power away without your permission.
Think about that. You voluntarily give it up in many ways and you're
most likely unaware of when and how you do it.

This behavior is likely not newly acquired. But now it's especially
important to change the pattern. Whether in meetings when you let
others take credit for your ideas, or when you remain silent and don't
offer your opinions, or in any number of other seemingly inconse-
quential actions, you might be giving away your power every day.
Chances are you feel powerless not because of any dramatic turn of

events. But like a fully inflated balloon that gradually loses air, you leak power slowly, over time, until you suddenly realize you're depleted.

Alice Walker said, "The most common way people give up their power is by thinking they don't have any." If you believe that as you age you lose power, then you'll no longer have power. And as a result, you'll put yourself in a subservient position that makes it super-easy for you to be steamrolled. So, my message to you is if you've been giving your power away for decades, now is the time to stop. You're more vulnerable than ever to being labeled expendable and stripped of your power at work. Don't let that happen.

At one point in my career, I gave up my power to a boss who was an intimidating, male chauvinist bully. Physically imposing compared with my petite frame, he had a regular speaking voice that was glass shattering. I could feel myself shrink in his presence, my stomach full of butterflies. When he gave me a direction I had an issue with, I wouldn't say a thing. I tried my best to avoid him. Of course, neither he nor his colleagues were witness to my thought processes and knowledge. The result was that I ended up missing out on a promotion for which I was highly qualified.

What are some of the ways you give your power away? Ask yourself:

- Do I let people take credit for my ideas?

- Do I let people talk over me?

- Do I compromise myself to be liked/accepted by younger colleagues?

- Do I make fun of my "senior moments"?

- Do I hold back about how I feel when they make nasty comments about my age? ("You were around with George Washington, right?" "Oh, look at you on Snapchat!" "You're such a mom.")

- Do I let people dismiss and ignore me?

- Do I not stand up for myself?

The first step in taking back your power is to be aware of just how you're surrendering it. Keep a diary of when you feel powerless and what triggers you to give up power. Note certain people or situations that cause you to pull back or play small. Look at the list and ask yourself what the consequences are for giving up your power in these ways. Then plan to take it back:

Behavior: I let people take credit for my ideas.

Consequence: People will keep doing this and I'll never be recognized for these ideas. I am more likely to lose out on promotions or lose my job.

What can I do: Comment in the meeting that I'm pleased that whoever repeated my idea thinks my idea is good. [This is taking back the power and recognition.] Make a pact with a coworker to acknowledge each other's ideas in meetings.

Carol, one of my former clients, also felt powerless with her male boss. He reminded her of her abusive father. She felt like a child in her interactions with him and feared being punished. She avoided him. Once she realized this and the consequences of her behavior, she learned to stand up for herself, engage as an equal, and let him know her thoughts and ideas instead of remaining silent. At first it was scary for her, but she consciously decided to maintain her power, and over time her interactions with him became easier.

Another one of my clients, Rita, an attorney at a large tech company, was one of the oldest in her department at fifty-eight. Her manager marginalized her. He limited her responsibilities and didn't invite her to critical meetings, all the while telling her she'd be okay. What the hell did that mean, *she'd be okay*? Did he mean she had job security? Was he insinuating that her status wouldn't change despite the fact she was clearly being left out and pushed aside? Nothing about her work felt right and Rita began to withdraw. Her demeanor changed. Her normally assertive tone became more passive as she feared for her job. She no longer openly offered her opinions and ideas. She stopped confronting her boss about being left out of key conversations. Every day that she acted this way, she was slowly giving away her power and appearing less valuable in the process.

Maybe someone once rolled their eyes after you commented in a meeting and you vowed never to open your mouth again because you took it personally and were humiliated. Who really loses here? Why give that person all your power?

The first step is to be aware of when you give your power away and the second step is to shift your thinking and develop more confidence in the face of obstacles and situations that trigger you. Keep track of this in your journal:

Action: Joe rolled his eyes when I commented during a meeting.

Reaction: I was embarrassed and vowed never to bring up anything in a meeting again.

Reflection: Joe has won. His eye-rolling silenced me and robbed me of my power. The consequence is that my silence will be misinterpreted as me having zero ideas or opinions to offer and this won't bode well when I'm evaluated.

Future action: [After recognizing how you've given up your power and the consequences, prepare yourself to face this ongoing challenge.] Joe has a right to his opinion and if he doesn't agree with me, that's fine. Although I welcome constructive criticism, he's being rude and I'm rising above it by sticking with what I think is a good point and standing in my power. I will speak up in meetings regardless of the eye-rolling. If I'm really feeling my oats, I also have the option of calling him out and asking him directly what he has a problem with. "I can't help but notice, Joe, that you don't seem to agree. What's your opinion on this?" [Badass move. Bet he won't do it again.]

What makes you feel empowered? Write a list in your journal. Here are some examples:

- I feel empowered when I am prepared and knowledgeable about a topic and I feel confident about asking good questions and making good points.

- I feel empowered when my opinions are respected and acknowledged.

- I feel empowered when people ask me for my opinion or for advice.

What are you doing when you feel powerful? Who are you with? Hold on to that feeling. Visualize what it would be like to feel that way at work. Own it.

Don't let the jerks at work bring you down. Remember *you* are the one giving up your power and only you can take it back.

I'll Never Get Another Job

SUSAN TOLD ME in confidence that she actively tries to hide her age with Botox and fillers. And she won't go into the office on her birthday for fear that someone will ask her how old she is. In the fashion industry, where a woman's appearance is always under a microscope, Susan is worried about her future: "I've been in this emotional slump but for no reason other than my own anxiety. It's the fear of *Holy shit, I'm sixty-two years old,* and excuse my French, but *who the f**k is going to hire me if I lose my job?* And it's this gripping fear."

Okay, there's some justification for Susan's fear. I'm not going to lie. The struggle for women to find a job after fifty is a major challenge and research confirms it. Studies have been done using fictitious résumés with phony graduation dates and the callback rates for middle-aged applicants were pathetically low, and even lower for middle-aged women. The biggest fear for older women who are being compromised, terminated, or forced to quit is that they're no longer considered employable.

If you're traumatized by this fear, you need to know that even though it's a challenge to find another job at this age, that doesn't mean you should adopt a victim mentality or curl up in fetal position for months and give up. Regardless of the circumstances behind your job loss, refuse to let the situation sabotage your future.

I want to tell you two different true stories to illustrate a point.

Laura was fifty years old when she was forced out of her position as managing director at a global financial institution. Although youthful and hip for her age, she was frequently referred to as a "dinosaur" and subjected to nasty comments from her younger female colleagues. She noticed she was losing credibility with her boss. He found more reasons to criticize her and fewer reasons to acknowledge her good work. Fewer client opportunities were sent her way. The company gave her some bogus reason that they were letting her go because they were consolidating, but Laura knew better. It was age discrimination. Twenty-two years of excellent performance didn't matter. The firm offered her a package and Laura took it, but the experience shook her to her core.

Anyone who experienced this might be traumatized. I mean, holy crap. Being dismissed so cavalierly after decades of great work sucks. It sucks big-time. It's a major-league suck. No question. And we all react differently to something like this. It certainly could have sidelined Laura and triggered fears about not getting another comparable job. But that's not how Laura let the situation play out. She pulled herself together. She started running and lost weight, which not only changed her appearance but improved her damaged self-esteem too. This newly gained confidence allowed her to refocus her energy on her future and put the negative emotions she was feeling behind her. And guess what? She landed another great job with a company that appreciates her contributions and she's at top of her game again. Go Laura! You're an inspiration to us all.

Now let's compare Laura's story to Janet's. Janet was an attorney at a large national law firm with headquarters in New York City. At sixty-three, she was downsized and devastated. A single mom with two kids in college, she quickly took another position with the federal government in DC as a program manager. She needed the salary and benefits. But now she's stuck. She hasn't been promoted in her government job and can't figure out how to get back to her previous status. On our brief call, I suggested several ideas about networking with former colleagues and using LinkedIn, as well as how to position herself for the future. But she had a reason why each suggestion I offered wouldn't work. Unwilling to try anything to move forward, she's digging herself into a hole without knowing it and, sadly, creating her own dead end.

Now whose example will you follow: Laura's empowered story of getting back on her feet and moving forward or Janet's tale of woe? Both women are highly qualified, but one is holding herself back. The obvious lesson here is that despite the challenge for women fifty-plus to find employment, your mindset about landing a new job is critical and can make the difference between success and failure.

Hear me out on this. If you tell yourself you'll *never* get another job, understand how that will influence your chances to get a job. Words have meaning and they affect your mindset and behavior. "Never" is a dangerous word. It is a dead end and it fuels a victim mentality. If you believe you'll never get another job after you've been let go, believe me, you'll never get a job. Or at the very best, it will take a great deal of time and angst to secure one.

If this is your assumption and fear, recognize it for what it is and understand the power this belief has over your future success. It may take some time to secure another job. It will take your commitment and dedication to work your network and look for opportunities. You need to stay optimistic. Persist for the positive and resist the negative.

Why wouldn't you do everything in your control to position yourself to succeed? That includes pushing aside your fear in favor of a can-do attitude. You may be turned down for a few jobs because of your age. That's been illegal since the Age Discrimination in Employment Act (ADEA) of 1967, and companies may claim you're overqualified or some other bullshit excuse, but don't let that distract you. Keep a laser focus on the value you bring to a prospective employer. You need to believe in yourself, sister. They'd be lucky to have you.

I'm Terrified
of Aging

WHEN YOU'RE FEARFUL of aging, you don't step into your full power and potential. In your head, the yellow caution light is always blinking: slow down, be careful, don't take on too much at once. This prevents you from taking risks, even calculated ones. Your manager could offer you an awesome assignment with a high-profile client that requires extensive international travel and your fear kicks in. Maybe you show some concern that you won't have the stamina or be up for the task at hand. You hesitate to take on this great opportunity because you fear that it requires you to expend too much energy and you believe that conserving your energy is critical at your age. What are you saving your energy for, if not for opportunities to live to the fullest each day? Conserving energy may be appropriate for someone over ninety, but you're not there yet.

Here's my point about fear: often it is more debilitating than the thing we're most afraid of.

I was terrified of menopause. To me it was the big "red line," and once I crossed it, I'd no longer feel sexy or be attractive to a man. The thought of not being able to have more children made me sad. Not that I wanted more, by the way. I was very pleased with the two

I had. But the choice was no longer there. And truth be told, after fifty-four years, forty-one of which were tied to tampons, I was sick of dealing with my period every month. Yet to me, menopause was this ominous and terrifying experience that I started obsessing about as I approached fifty. I built up all this anxiety about the unknown beforehand. I mourned the loss of my sexiness and youth, and was frightened about what would happen during and post-menopause. Hindsight being 20/20, that fear was a total waste of my energy. Period.

I believed that menopause was the beginning of the end, and the rest was all downhill. What would it be like? Would I have disabling hot flashes at work? Would my vagina dry up? Would I lose my libido?

No getting around it, menopause does mark the end of having children. And many women are debilitated by depression, foggy thinking, hot flashes, and loss of libido. I consider myself incredibly fortunate that I had none of those symptoms. Sure, my bones started to crave estrogen and I developed osteopenia and went on bioidentical hormone cream. But now I'm strong and sexy, healthy and happy. And there's a tremendous sense of freedom post-menopause. No worry about how you'll make it through work on the first day of your period. No more cramps or hormone-related headaches. And without a doubt, sex is wonderfully enjoyable *sans* the worry of getting pregnant. Whoopee! That alone is a reason to celebrate. Another benefit of aging. Don't ever take better sex for granted.

All the fears and assumptions I had about menopause were more debilitating than going through it. Here's the big takeaway: assumptions can be crippling on their own. And this is backed by science. Yale researchers found that a group of people aged fifty and above who had positive self-perceptions about getting older lived seven and a half years longer than people who expressed less positive attitudes about aging. The Negative Nancys were twice as likely to experience a heart attack or stroke than those with positive outlooks. Other studies confirm that when you believe that everything's going to get worse as you age, that mindset affects your health, such as developing changes in your brain and the onset of Alzheimer's disease.

Do I have your attention here? You can control how you age to some degree. Accept the reality with grace and don't let fear disable you more than the aging process itself. I often remind myself that I don't want any regrets at the end of my life. What a waste of time it is to be anxious and worried about aging instead of living. You only get one chance at this, sister.

We don't know what our next chapters will bring. Why do we always assume the worst? Yes, we'll eventually slow down and we won't be able to run a seven-minute mile anymore (I never even came close to that when I was twenty) or remember the lyrics to that song by what's his name. But aging is a natural process and we're lucky to be alive, to have the opportunity to age.

Each day is a new adventure and opportunity to experience joy. We may need glasses to see the beauty around us more clearly and hearing aids to listen to the subtle sounds of nature. But we're here, damn it! As Ram Dass reminded us, "Be here now."

Part Two

STOP PLAYING SMALL, AND DO WHAT IT TAKES TO STAY IN THE GAME

I've had a pretty successful career. No complaints. I managed to navigate male-dominated workplaces, ride the wave of terminations and find new jobs, climb the ladder to the C-suite, and start my own coaching business. My twenty-plus-year corporate career taught me many valuable lessons about what it takes for a woman to get ahead and stay ahead, many of which are included in my book *The Politics of Promotion*. The lessons apply to all generations of ambitious women in the workplace.

One of the most important things I've learned over the years is how vital it is to think strategically and take control of your career trajectory. It doesn't matter whether you're just starting out, you're mid-career, or you're approaching retirement. You can't sit on your ass and wait for things to miraculously happen for you. You can't sit on your ass and wait for the other shoe to drop. Curling up in a ball and playing the victim won't work either. The only person you can count on at the end of the day is you. Sure, other people can open doors for you and introduce you to new opportunities. But you alone decide whether or not to follow through. You alone control whether or not to push aside self-doubt and put yourself out there. You control your attitude. You control whether or not you take control.

All the chapters in this section offer you my best coaching advice about how to stay marketable and keep your job. Although this advice is essential throughout your career, it is a necessary and critical tune-up now that you're over fifty and more vulnerable than ever to being sidelined and/or pushed out the door.

The lessons in these chapters assist you to take control of your career and do so now—not once you're downsized or pushed out, but now. Be proactive. Step up your skills. Your future and financial viability are on the line, and I'm here to help you every step of the way.

Declare Your
Ambition

I'M NOT SURE when ambition became taboo for women. But there
seems to be a kind of unwritten rule that women shouldn't own
up to being ambitious or they'll be labeled a nasty bitch who steps
on anyone in her way to get ahead. Bear in mind, it's perfectly acceptable—in fact, expected—that men be ambitious. That's a double
standard that comes from our patriarchal society. I'm not going to go
on a rant and let myself be distracted about that here, because I could
write a whole book on the topic, but my point is that most women end
up hiding their ambition and playing small to be accepted and liked.
You can't afford to make this compromise.

If you've never come out of the closet as ambitious (god forbid),
you'd better do it now. That doesn't mean stomping around the office
telling everyone, "Hey, I just wanted to let you know I'm ambitious,"
like some kind of late-to-the-party confessional. Ambition doesn't
necessarily mean having a lofty goal of being in the C-suite, although
that's perfectly acceptable if that's your gig. But declaring your ambition does mean letting others know that you have every intention of
continuing your career with the same energy and commitment that
you've always demonstrated. And this is super-important because
when you pass fifty, most people are going to assume otherwise.

Listen up. You've got to debunk the assumptions your colleagues and managers are most likely making about you at this stage in your career. The general ageist consensus is that older employees, especially women over fifty, no longer have the interest in or stamina to work. Mind you, this assumption has been widely disputed by research that shows older workers are just as motivated and reliable as their younger colleagues *and* surpass their job performance. But don't count on anyone paying attention to that. It is your responsibility to let your manager know you're still in the game and have no intention of retiring in the next few years.

The majority of women over fifty are still ambitious and don't want to retire, despite assumptions to the contrary. In fact, my research in this area revealed a rise in ambition for women in this age demographic. Their motivation isn't always financial. They seek fulfilling work and want to apply their skills and experience and remain in the workplace as long as possible, or they decide to start their own businesses. Is this where you're at? Yes, maybe you're frustrated that you are no longer valued at work. If circumstances in the workplace were better, these years would be your most satisfying. And you still have a lot to contribute; you want to be productive. So—no bullshit here—you've got to let others know that you are not going to slow down any time soon. I'm telling you this straight. You've got to let the powers that be know they can count on you going forward. You're in it with gusto.

Tell your manager that you're ready, willing, and able to do your best work. Don't assume they already know that. They're most likely assuming that you don't want to work too hard and have lost your grit. Prove them wrong! Schedule a meeting with your boss and let them know what you'd like to discuss so they're not blindsided: "I'd like to get together to talk about how I can best continue to contribute value to you, my team, and this organization. When are you available to sit down and discuss?"

Prepare for the meeting. Review your accomplishments since you have been at the company or under their management, and be prepared to articulate how you plan to support their objectives going forward.

Here's an example: "I've built strong relationships and influence, not only in this department but across the organization, to help sell your initiatives and ideas. I know the company will be going through some changes in the next few years. What role do you see for me going forward? How can I best add value? I'm committed to doing my best work now and in the future." You're invested and want to continue to contribute value to the company.

Work together to create a career path for the next few years. Maybe you stay in the department or maybe there are other opportunities for you that your manager can suggest. State your value and ask. And don't make this a quiet, tentative, mousy kind of ask. Be bold and state your intention.

Maybe you have a specific position or promotion as your goal. Share that with your manager as well and discuss the best path for you to achieve that goal. Do you need to improve certain skills? Do you need more experience in a certain area and can they help you get that? In other words, how do you get from where you are now to where you'd like to be? If you're happy in your current job and want to make sure that you have a future in that role, let your manager know that staying in this role is your goal. Solicit their feedback on the best way to continue to contribute value in the next few years.

Demonstrate that you're still committed to the work. Kate was not only the oldest one on the trading floor but also the only woman: "It bothered me to be the oldest one because I was afraid of facing round two of what I'd faced as a woman in this environment, just in a different context. Now I'm an old woman in this environment and people are just assuming that I'm killing time. So, I tried not to slow down in my work effort, to be on top of everything, to just be as informed and smart as I could be so that no one could claim, 'Oh, she's slipping. She's old now.'"

Here's my best advice. Show up every day as a team player. Do your best work. Debunk any ageist assumptions that you're on your way out by articulating your value. Let everyone who matters know you're still a key player and that you intend to support your boss, your team, and your company going forward. Ambition doesn't end on a particular birthday. Own it and live it.

Advocate for Yourself and Others

HEADS UP, GIRLFRIEND. Here's some important advice. Never ever discount the importance of advocating for yourself, especially as a woman, especially as an older woman. Come on, I shouldn't even have to tell you this. You know it already. You see this play out every day. The people who've got this down get ahead, plain and simple. They're visible, everyone knows about their work and, most importantly, the results they get. Why? Because they let people know what they're doing and how they're doing it, in a savvy way that doesn't piss anyone off.

What the hell? Why don't we all do this? Why do we stay silent instead of letting people know about our accomplishments? We've got a boatload of baggage about self-promotion, that's why. It's bragging, and no one will like us if we brag. We feel phony and cheap if we attempt it, so we don't. Chances are we were brought up with the idea that we should be humble and wait to be recognized. Yeah, all the messages that were directed at us, not our brothers, and that we sucked in and took to heart. We've been brainwashed to believe that bragging is bad when, in fact, it's badass. In response to these messages, we've gone to the extreme. We don't brag about ourselves and we're not even comfortable sharing our accomplishments. Then we wonder why we get passed over and why we are not recognized and rewarded for our work. Duh!

A devil's advocate could argue that if you were effectively speaking up for yourself all along, you wouldn't be compromised now as an older woman. Perhaps that's true, but let's not go there. What's important is the present and your future. It's never too late to create more visibility and credibility for yourself. If you're being marginalized now, make sure you don't completely fall off the radar or get pushed off the cliff. This is critical for you to stay in the game.

The best way to start learning effective self-promotion is by identifying your value proposition. Your value proposition is how your work contributes to positive business outcomes. Unlike your job description, your value proposition describes how you achieve results and what those results mean to the company. This gives you a platform to position yourself as someone who can help others reach their objectives. What does your manager hope to achieve? What are the department's goals? What is the mission of the company? Use your value proposition to let others know how you can assist them in reaching their goals. It instantly gives you visibility along with credibility, which, I want to remind you, you need.

Unlike a formal elevator pitch, when you talk about your value proposition, you aren't memorizing a generic message that no one listens to or cares about and that gives you the heebie-jeebies to recite. You observe others, ask questions, and listen to learn what's important to them. And then you let them know how you help. By doing this, you earn a reputation as someone who is committed to the work and the company, and as someone who is not easily dismissed.

Identify key stakeholders and influencers and build relationships with them, using your value proposition to position yourself as someone who can contribute for the benefit of the company. For example, "I understand that you've been challenged to complete your projects in a timely fashion and that's dramatically affected your ability to hit

your numbers. Perhaps I can help. My ability to build strong relationships of trust with the team, motivate, and hold them accountable has
resulted in my projects beating deadlines, increasing customer satisfaction, and adding to the bottom line." This is a win-win relationship.
Remember you're a badass player here. You've got lots of great stuff to
offer. And you need to remind them.

When I was newly divorced with two young children, I needed to
find a job that paid more than my kindergarten teaching job. I wasn't
sure where to start but I looked in the want ads in the local paper.
Remember those? Anyway, I found an ad for a medical secretary with
a large physician group in Danbury, Connecticut, which was close to
where I was living. I assumed that my BA in sociology and graduate
degree in education would help me get a job, but of course the opposite happened. They told me that I was too qualified and they feared I'd
be bored with the job and leave in a couple of months. I tried to assure
them, just short of pleading with them, that I needed the job and that
would never happen. They didn't believe me. I didn't get the job.

Here's the thing, though. I obviously made a great impression
because a couple of weeks later they called me and asked if I wanted
to interview for the job of administrator at a new cardiac rehab joint
venture they were opening with about thirty doctors, a position for
which I had zero qualifications. I barely knew how to balance my
checkbook. I know, I know. It's hard to believe that any thirty-four-
year-old was that inept. But I'm ashamed to say it was true at the time.

Anyway, I interviewed and got the job despite having no relevant
experience. But here's what's important. I did it by promoting myself
well, not going on and on about how qualified I was, because that
would have been an outright lie. I had only teaching experience at
that point. But I figured out what was important to them. They wanted
someone who was comfortable working with doctors, someone who
wouldn't be intimidated and could hold the doctors accountable for
completing their paperwork, and so on. I let them know that I came

from a medical family, my community growing up included physicians, and that to me, doctors were just people, not gods.

Also, my father had had a heart attack when he was fifty-seven and I was familiar with the cardiac rehab world. He dramatically changed his diet and started a rigorous exercise program. Our whole family adopted his new lifestyle. I was living it. And here was the icing on the cake: I was teaching aerobic dancing at the time. (Remember this fad, ladies?) I was passionate about cardiac fitness and I aligned my values with their values, and that nailed it. For them, teaching me the business was the easy part. They knew I was smart. They assumed I was teachable. So, there you have it. They gave me the job, trained me well, and in a year and a half I was running eleven centers for them up and down the East Coast. It was my entry into business.

The lesson here about self-advocacy is that you need to understand what's important to your company or boss or colleagues and connect the dots between what you bring to the table and what they want and need. And voilà. It's magic. You're advocating for yourself by letting them know how your work can help them reach their objectives. It's mutually beneficial. You get the visibility and credit for your work and they get what they need.

Along with these internal conversations, try promoting yourself on social media. Don't be shy. Everybody does it. Share all your wins. It's actually easier to do this online than in person, so take advantage of your LinkedIn, Facebook, Instagram, and Twitter accounts to brag about yourself. For instance, you may post a picture of you and your team having a celebratory lunch after kicking ass with a new campaign. You may write a post about how honored you are to have received a certain award for increased sales. And don't pay attention to any naysayers who try to knock you down. That's all part of the social media game.

Subha Barry, senior vice president and managing director of Working Mother Media, previously worked in financial services, where women lack visibility and are often passed over because of it. She and some of her female colleagues made a pact to advocate for each other on a regular basis and help each other get the recognition they deserved. A brag club. Uncomfortable with self-promotion as individuals, they would meet monthly and share their accomplishments with one another, with the intention of spreading the word across the company. Then, the following month, they would meet again and update each other, continuing their commitment to talk up their colleagues. This is such a great idea. Form a brag club with your women colleagues and help each other out.

Advocating for each other internally is powerful, but you also want to team up with your colleagues to promote one another on social media. Provide testimonials on LinkedIn, agree to tweet about each other's accomplishments, and share and like posts on Instagram. Don't be stingy with your praise and support of other women. What goes around comes around. It's great karma.

If you're on a team that has a small percentage of women, form a coalition to recognize each other in meetings. There is no greater example of this than what the women in the West Wing of the White House did during the Obama administration. Female staffers who had a seat at the table but were often overlooked adopted a meeting strategy they called "amplification." When a woman raised a key point, other women would repeat it, giving credit to its author. This strategy forced the men in the room to recognize the contribution—and denied them the opportunity to claim the idea as their own. Because, let's face it, men automatically seem to grab the credit most of the time.

Here are some great tips for keeping track of all the super stuff you're doing to fuel your confidence and self-advocacy.

Keep a success journal of your accomplishments

Picture this: you're driving home from work, thinking about your day, and you begin to beat yourself up for things you didn't do or could've done better. *That was so stupid of me to bring up that point in the meeting. It was so obvious no one cared about it. What a jerk I am. Now I'll never get the raise I want and maybe I'll even get fired because everyone knows I'm stupid. This could be the end of my career . . .* Sound familiar?

Why did I let that asshole, John, take credit for my great idea? I just sat there in silence. What the hell's wrong with me? When am I going to learn not to be a doormat? I always let people step all over me and no one has any respect for me and I'm just never going to ever say anything in a meeting again. And I definitely need some chocolate right about now . . .

I could've done a much better job with my presentation today. I should've had more slides to explain things better. I just never seem to get it right. I should have spent more time doing research. I cut corners and everyone knew it and I'm a failure . . .

I could go on and on because we always, and I mean always, have these conversations with ourselves about how we f**k up. When we're thinking about our day, we consistently go negative. It's our default. Rarely do we pat ourselves on the back and congratulate ourselves for doing anything right. And because of that, we forget. Yes, we forget all the good stuff that we've done. Our memory of it gets drowned out because we're expending all our energy beating ourselves up for sins we may or may not have committed.

Because of our tendency to go negative, we need to find a way to celebrate the good things we do. Now you may be saying to yourself, *What great things?* The fact that you may not easily recall your accomplishments just reinforces the need to keep a success journal.

This is what I want you to do: buy a journal, a nice journal, and a pen. You can find some beautiful journals at book or stationery stores. Buy something you love. At the end of every day, I want you to write down at least one thing, big or small, that you accomplished that day. Any accomplishment qualifies:

- I had an important conversation with a customer today that helped close the deal.

- I complimented my colleague on her contribution to the project we're working on.

- My persistence chasing a cold lead paid off and we have a new customer.

At the end of the week, I want you to review your entries and then ask yourself, *What does all this say about me?*

- My influential conversations and persistence help to close deals and increase revenue.

- My ability to sustain strong relationships with my team helps to keep them motivated and productive so we successfully finish projects on time.

- I'm pretty awesome and I add a lot of value to my company.

Got it?

Over time, your positive journal entries will reinforce your "atta girl" thinking. By the way, I'm not just making this stuff up. Science confirms that a repeated and consistent practice of positive thinking can change the neural pathways in your brain so you're not always a Debbie Downer. Trust me on this. That's a great benefit that we all can use.

But what's super-important about the success journal is that it allows you to stay in touch with all your accomplishments, many of which you would probably forget over the course of the year. The success journal gives you the ability to better understand your value proposition as well as the confidence to advocate for yourself. After doing this for a while, you'll own what you bring to the table.

Write a weekly status report for your manager

Another great way to advocate for yourself is to write a weekly status report for your manager. I coach all my clients to do this. Certainly, your manager can't keep track of everything you're doing. Everyone is so super-busy these days they can barely recollect their own accomplishments, let alone yours. The status report is the perfect method to keep your boss in the loop and to record the feedback you need to be successful. Sending the report before your one-on-one meeting lets them know what you've been up to and provides an agenda for your meeting together. Then the report itself is an ongoing record of everything you've done and serves as a foolproof reference tool for your year-end performance review and your self-evaluation. Most managers welcome this information. Besides being an excellent vehicle for your recognition, it makes their job easier.

Here's a sample template. Just repeat for each project you're working on and add in final results when each project is complete.

Week ending: _____

Project 1: _____

Accomplishments so far: _____

_____

_____

Ongoing challenges: _____

_____

_____

Feedback: _____

_____

_____

Even thinking about self-advocacy can cause most of us to break out in hives. We hate doing it and we generally suck at it. But identifying your value proposition and tying that to supporting others in the workplace gives you the visibility and credibility you need to stay marketable and keep your job. It's a powerful way to advocate for yourself without coming across as a braggart.

Use social media to announce your accomplishments as well as those of your colleagues. And form a brag club to help each other out. Make a deal with your trusted female colleagues to call out the jerks who take credit for your stuff. Keep a success journal to fuel your confidence and to record all the great things you're doing, and last, but not least, write a weekly status report for your boss to send before your regular meetings, and use its content to gain credibility.

You've got this. It's time to give yourself credit and let others know you deserve to be where you are. It's never too late to own your talent, experience, and accomplishments and claim your rightful place in the company.

Build a Cross-Generational Network

YOU MAY FEEL isolated at work because of your age. When you look around your department and company, is it possible that you're the only mother or grandmother? Maybe for years you've felt awkward being the only woman at the table and now you're the only woman *and* the oldest. I've been told that in many tech companies today, you're considered old once you have children. Geez. If you're considered a dinosaur at thirty, what does that say about those of us over fifty?

But here's the reality: we put people in categories based on their age and then make assumptions about them. Of course, we also do this with gender, religion, education, sexual orientation, race. It seems to be human nature. However, all these assumptions separate us. They keep us from interacting and getting to know one another. We are blinded by our own biases.

So, it's understandable that we hold ourselves back from getting to know anyone who's different. It's not really comfortable for either party. We assume things about younger people and they have their own thoughts about us. And let me be clear: it's much easier to stay safe with our assumptions and stereotypes than to connect with people who aren't just like us—in this case, our colleagues who may even be younger than our kids. Yet assumptions and stereotypes melt away when we reach out and get to know people personally.

At this stage of your career, however, you can't afford to isolate yourself. You can't afford to be lumped into a category that's headed out to pasture. You need your colleagues to know you personally and thereby learn to appreciate your experience and wisdom, and you aren't going to be able to make this happen unless you connect across the generational gap. After all, some workplaces have six generations working together. And most likely, you're in one of the *older* generations, which could mean virtually all your colleagues are younger than you. Yikes! How's that for a reality check? On the positive side, however, that just means that you potentially have a very large network.

When you think about reaching out to younger colleagues, questions arise. *What do we have in common? Why would they even want to talk to me? Wouldn't they think it's a waste of time? Won't they just laugh and dismiss me as irrelevant and useless?* Perhaps. But remember this: building a cross-generational network benefits everyone, and for you, it busts the ageist myth that you're too set in your ways and not invested in your work. Expanding your horizon and getting to know your younger teammates to better understand what makes them tick is simply a good practice.

Now, I'm not saying it's always easy. How do you even find these people? Where do you begin? Well, certainly you have junior coworkers on your team or in your department. That's a great place to start to build relationships, because they already kind of know you. Look also to join different affinity groups, as they will also give you exposure across generations, and you already have something in common with the members or you wouldn't become involved in the group to begin with.

Reach out and plan a lunch or coffee with a young colleague with the goal of learning more about them, their background, their goals, their challenges. What do they want and need to be successful and how can you help? How can they help you? This is all about win-win situations. Create mutually beneficial relationships, where your expertise in one area would be helpful and, in turn, you develop a new skill, like learning the ins and outs of Instagram or TikTok. You never know what will happen until you start conversations.

I don't know about your company, but in many workplaces, social activities are consciously or unconsciously organized to exclude older women. One woman I spoke with shared that sometimes an all-office email goes out inviting everyone to the bar across the street for happy hour: "But it's not like they're really going to seek you out when it's just a small group, because you're not their peer. And so you kind of miss out on some of the office culture, the office fun. When you're older in a young environment, it just feels off. Sometimes team-building physical activities are geared to younger employees and the assumption is that you're not fit enough to participate. You feel like an outsider, an outcast."

Attend some of these activities if you can. Casual get-togethers are a great way to get to know people outside the work environment. If it turns out to be painful and a total waste of time, just drop in and say hi without staying for the duration. It shows you're trying. And that effort counts for something. If you feel excluded from certain organized events, suggest different types of activities that might appeal to a broad audience: concerts, plays, lectures, a restaurant opening. Take the initiative. Be the organizer. Make it inclusive.

Most likely, your junior coworkers are just beginning their careers and are ambitious. They're hungry to build their networks and learn from some experienced people. If you're at an event and there's someone you know in the room, introduce a young colleague to them. Beyond networking events, connect them to business acquaintances and colleagues who could help them. Let's face it, you've been around the block more than a couple of times and you know a lot of people.

And helping younger people build their network can pay dividends for you. They can introduce you not only to others but also potentially to new ideas and opportunities that an expansive, diverse network affords you. You might even discover that younger people will gravitate to you if they see you as someone who will open doors and make key introductions for them.

Perhaps you could mimic the influential women of seventeenth- and eighteenth-century Paris, who hosted salons for other women inside private hotels or mansions and outside the limitations of a male-dominated society. Here young women had the opportunity to learn how best to navigate society with elegance and poise. They were introduced to the great intellectuals of the time and had a safe haven to express themselves freely.

What if you offered a similar opportunity for young women to gather and meet influential people? To brainstorm and talk through the challenges of being an ambitious young woman? What if you held these salons on a regular basis to discuss these topics or books of interest? You can do this with the company's blessing or privately. Either way, you're making strong connections with young women and positioning yourself as an influential force. I could get used to my role as Madame Marcus, the patron of young talented women. Couldn't you?

And don't forget, as you build these personal relationships, people get to know who you are and no longer see you as a stereotype of an older woman. They see you as a player, as someone who's valuable to them. And you reap the rewards as well. This is what you want and need to stay relevant! And I might add that connecting people for mutual benefit is energizing. It's one of my favorite things to do. Once you try it, I'm sure you'll learn to love it too, if for no other reason than you feel useful. A network is an asset and if you can help your young colleagues build theirs, you're in the game, girlfriend.

Mentor Others, and Find One for Yourself While You're at It

I'VE BEEN LUCKY to have some great mentors over the course of my career. Mind you, none were ever formal mentors but powerful female role models who took the time to have impactful conversations with me. They showed me the ropes, helped me navigate some tough challenges, opened doors, and awakened me to opportunities I didn't see on my own. No question about it, mentors helped me shape my career. Most of these advisors were my managers. They were invested in my success and I owe them a ton of gratitude for helping me.

These women managers kicked ass in a male-dominated space. Early in my career, two in particular, Kathy V. and Judy J., helped me by example. They were unapologetic about their boldness and confidence and had no problem whatsoever challenging the status quo when they had the power of their convictions behind them. Great role models. I watched the way they spoke directly to the CEO, often putting him in his place without paying the price. I observed closely how they presented their business case to key stakeholders in meetings, and how they refused to back down when confronted. Their arguments had no fluff. They relied on numbers and data and common sense. They often won the point as a result. Their refusal to bow to the convention that women need to be timid and agreeable earned them respect from the CEO and other leaders across the company. And, most important to mention here, they each had a great sense of humor and didn't take everything personally or seriously. They didn't take shit from anyone either. They knew how to work hard and play hard. And play hard we did. I learned the importance of balancing my work and my young family. Don't get me wrong, it wasn't always hunky-dory. Sometimes they gave me tough feedback that was direct and bold as well, but they never held back the praise when I accomplished something. And that's "a somethin'," as Roseanne Roseannadanna used to say.

You can provide this same type of guidance for a young coworker. Be that role model. Offer advice and share the experiences you've had and the wisdom you've gleaned over the years. You want to stay relevant, right? Create visibility for yourself? Add value? Avoid being pushed out the door? Be a mentor. It serves many purposes. You show you're in the game and committed to the organization. You gain visibility for the value you offer and you build relationships with younger employees, from whom you can learn a lot as well.

Where do you find an appropriate mentee? You may not need to look further than your team. And as you're building your internal network, you might want to offer to informally mentor a young colleague. Schedule a monthly coffee or lunch for starters. Get to know them and be curious. What are some of their challenges? Can you help? Get the word out to your manager and others in the organization that you would welcome an opportunity to mentor.

Find out if your company has a formal mentorship program. Who's in charge? How does it work? Let the powers that be know you'd like to get involved. Even if there's no formal mentorship program, contact human resources and let them know that, as someone who's more seasoned and knows the ropes, you're willing to mentor a younger employee. The relationship can be formal or informal, where you serve more as an advisor and role model. Human resources can help you find a mentee even outside your department.

Are you feeling some resistance to this? Perhaps you're fearful of mentoring a younger employee who may be promoted before you or take your job some day and push you out. This is always a possibility; sometimes life ain't fair. But take the high road and be generous with your advice. You never know what that relationship may become over time. Maybe this person will become your manager, but perhaps they will also help you find a new job with a different company in the future.

Think about what skills and experiences might be valuable to share. Ask your manager about the possibility of setting up a lunch-and-learn session on a topic that would prove useful to others in your department or team. Or better yet, organize monthly lunch-and-learns where you highlight your expertise and you invite colleagues to do the same.

And for god's sake, don't shortchange yourself. Find your own mentor. It's never too late for the sound advice a mentor can offer. The type of advice you request and receive will be different from when you were starting your career, but the relationship itself doesn't change. You may find it helpful to look for someone who has learned how to survive and thrive over fifty. You may believe that the perspective a younger person can give you would be beneficial. Or you may choose both. Whether or not your mentor is from your company, their experience can help you.

You don't have to limit yourself to just one mentor or just women mentors. Create a personal advisory board of diverse people who represent different industries, experiences, age, ethnicities, and genders, who are willing to give you advice as well as their point of view. You never know what gems of wisdom you can pick up through these relationships.

Right about now you may be saying to yourself, *Who would want to mentor me at this stage of my career?* But just cut the crap, okay? Are you really going to sabotage an opportunity to gain insight into what it takes to sustain a career over time? Although you may be hesitant to ask someone for advice, don't automatically discount doing this. People are usually honored to be asked about how they became successful and are more than happy to talk about it. Let's face it, we all like to give advice. It's taking advice that's usually an issue.

My gut tells me that the more we need a mentor, the more we hesitate to look for one. What's that about? Embarrassed? Think we should know it all by this time in our career? That's bullshit.

One of my recent mentors is CEO of an international company. He frequently reminds me to stop playing small. Think big. Take risks (okay, calculated risks) and stop holding myself back. This is my weak spot. And I learn from his example and relish his encouragement. He holds me accountable for my behavior by calling me out when I wander off course and choose the path of least resistance.

Who can help you stay focused and hold you accountable? Where do you need some support and encouragement? Or do you need more of a shove? Tell your mentor what you need.

Being a mentor or mentee is good for your career at this point. You need to show your commitment. You need to be visible and build relationships across generations. So, make the time. Make the effort. Reach out. Do yourself a favor and get over yourself.

Raise Your Hand,
Share Your Ideas

WHEN I WAS in elementary school, I couldn't wait to raise my hand to answer a question and show how smart I was. *Ooo! Ooo! Call on me*, I'd think to myself as I struggled to get my hand higher in the air and more visible to the teacher. *Please call on me. I've got the answer.* Yeah, I was a bit precocious. Were you? Do you remember those days? Well, what the hell happened since then? Did we get dumb and dumber over the years? Did our brain cells shrivel up? Is it possible we never have good answers anymore? Or is it that we do have ideas to share but we hesitate to raise our hands? It's the latter for sure.

Maybe we aren't raising our hands because for years we've been ignored and easily dismissed. No question that only decades ago, women weren't thought of as equal in intelligence or ambition. We weren't given the recognition for our ideas even when we brought them forward. Gender bias was common and acceptable. I need to remind myself every now and then how bad it was in the late '80s and early '90s when I started my career. Men ruled. White men ruled. Wait a minute! They still do! But at least now society is becoming fairly savvy and recognizing that a diverse group of women have to be at the table if business is going to be profitable and ethical.

Now, however, we face the double whammy of being female and being older. Gender bias and ageism together. We're kind of back where we started, you know? People assume that at our age we're no longer intelligent or ambitious. How are you going to fight that? Show all the small-minded jerks that you have a brain, that's how. Raise your hand and share your ideas. I'm certain you've got some good ones in there. Go for it.

One of my pet peeves with myself is when I hold back and someone else makes the same point I was thinking of but couldn't quite spit out. People respond enthusiastically and nod their heads in approval. "Good idea," they say. "That's really smart." Well, I had that same idea. Guess what? That doesn't count. It doesn't count unless you're the one who speaks up. You can state that you agree, but that's second best to being the one who says it first.

Honestly, we can think of hundreds of reasons not to raise our hand and share our ideas, all of which stem from our insecurity and fear of being called out as stupid. Well, you're *not* stupid, but it is stupid to not volunteer your thoughts and opinions. When you remain silent, you become irrelevant, invisible, and you set yourself up to be marginalized.

So, prepare to speak up.

For your next meeting, I suggest the following:

- Get the agenda ahead of time and do your research. You'll feel much more confident when you understand the topic and the history.

- Plan the best way to deliver and position your thoughts.

- Build consensus for your own idea with stakeholders and colleagues before the meeting to ensure a safe environment and platform, and also to get critical feedback before you open your mouth.

- Speak up and share your idea. You're giving the message that you're still in the game.

- Prepare good questions.

- Contribute to the discussion even if it's to agree with someone. Acknowledge someone else's idea.

- Add your own two cents about an idea on the table. Show an out-of-the-box, innovative approach. (It's considered valuable and even youthful.)

If you're not invited to the meeting but want to contribute:

- Learn about the meeting topic and agenda. Research if needed. Formalize some creative ideas.

- Let the organizer know that you'd like to attend and have some new ideas about the topic. You're giving the message that you still have value and won't be easily dismissed.

What you don't want to do is be a sourpuss in the office, feeling like a victim because you weren't invited to the meeting. Don't waste a minute going there. Seize the opportunity to put together your ideas and communicate them to gain admission to the meeting. If you still don't get invited, nothing's lost. You've at least set the stage to be asked to attend future meetings and you've gained credibility by sharing your ideas. Remember you have a wealth of experience to draw from and you're smart. Don't let negative thinking stop you from showing up as a valuable contributor because your feelings were hurt when you weren't included.

As you approach fifty and beyond, people may assume that you're stale and not hip to innovative thinking. They believe you're just biding your time until your time is up. Keep this in mind and say to yourself, *Not so fast. I still have years of great contributions to make.* Start making them today.

Be Visible

YOUR COLLEAGUES may make demeaning and humiliating comments to knock you down. Yeah, we've heard them all. "She's a dinosaur." "She's over the hill." Yada yada. We get it. You think you're better and smarter and more valuable because you're thirty, not sixty.

You hear rumblings that there's a plan to give part of your workload to someone younger. Your gut instinct warns you of danger if you put yourself out there. It's certainly easier to hide beneath the radar. That's called avoidance and it's not really safer. Because what does that get you? I'll tell you what it gets you: ignored and possibly shown the nearest exit. If you're off the radar and invisible, no one has any idea what value you contribute. How can you position yourself as a key player if you're hiding? So, if you really think that's a safer route, you're mistaken. You have a choice: Do you fade into the shadows of irrelevance or do you think strategically about how to be more visible? Your job is on the line, and the older you get, the wiser you need to be about this reality.

Let's talk about how to trade miserable for visible. Be positive and proactive. Think strategically and create a visibility plan to increase your profile and exposure across the organization. Record the plan in your journal.

Here are some ideas:

Volunteer for special projects. Volunteer for special projects that have visibility with senior leadership and influencers. You may need to do a little undercover work here if what's important to key stakeholders isn't obvious. Is there a new initiative they're trying to get off the ground? Look around. Ask around. Identify some projects that matter to the people in power. For example, maybe the organization is adopting a new IT system and people across the company are resisting the change. How can you help?

Volunteer for company-wide social activities. Volunteer to help with company social activities. What's on the company calendar this year? Could you organize some events? Get on a committee and be useful. It's a great way to meet people you would normally never encounter across the company.

Attend company social events. Get your ass out the door and go to some company events. I don't care if you aren't in the mood. Find a couple you can tolerate and go. And if you go, don't hang out in the corner with the Debbie Downers. Mingle. Smile. Be visible.

Arrange outings with colleagues. You can kvetch all you want that you don't like any of the social events, and in reality, some may not be a great fit. Bowling, pickleball, poker, golf? Ugh. So, organize something new that would appeal to everyone. Be a player.

Join an existing women's leadership group. Most companies have some sort of women's network or leadership group. Get involved. Sit on a committee. Build your community. In many cases, these groups have executive sponsors and visibility with them is just what you want and need.

Initiate a new women's leadership group. If your company doesn't have a woman's leadership group, put the word out to your boss and HR manager that you'd like to bring together a group of like-minded women to create one. Or identify a senior leader who'd be sympathetic to this initiative and reach out to them to sponsor the group. This is a great topic of discussion for networking, by the way. Run the idea by some women and see who's interested. Show initiative and leadership.

Initiate a community-based program for social good. Many companies have community outreach activities and programs, such as food pantry drives, blood drives, volunteer work with Boys and Girls Clubs, helping people with disabilities, food kitchens during holidays, and marches for different causes (including the annual Women's March). If you're passionate about a specific cause, organize an event and coordinate with local leaders.

Offer to mentor. Mentoring is a powerful and effective way to gain visibility, network, and build credibility. Reread the chapter on mentoring to refresh your thinking about where to start.

Start a cross-generational mentoring or networking program. If your company does not have a mentoring or networking program, initiate one. Promote the idea across the company to build interest. Work on getting leadership support and solicit the help of an executive sponsor. All these actions create visibility and demonstrate your leadership and ongoing engagement.

Host lunch-and-learns. We've talked about lunch-and-learns as an activity to showcase your skills and add value to your team. If no program like this exists, approach your manager to get buy-in, and solicit feedback from your team and department on topics, logistics, and so on. Set up a committee to vet speakers and topics, and put yourself forward as one of the speakers. I would dare anyone to question your commitment to your work and the company if you're spearheading an initiative like this.

Choose one or more of these actions. Got ideas of your own? Select one and then draft your plan of attack. Hold yourself accountable to thoroughly research the topic beforehand. Are there any existing community or company projects? What are they? Who's in charge? Can these be expanded? Your renewed visibility starts now. Take action!

Ask for
Feedback

OKAY. THIS MAY be really scary. Your manager may be younger than your children and perhaps you assume that they can't wait to push you out of their budget and off their team. Do you know that for sure? I bet not. Unless you have evidence to support that assumption, it's most likely your fear rearing its ugly head.

Wouldn't you prefer to know where you stand instead of being blindsided one day? If you meet with your manager on a regular basis and request feedback on how you're doing, you show you are dedicated to doing your best work. You're interested. Don't be afraid to solicit the information you need to position yourself appropriately.

I don't care how old you are, asking for feedback can be tricky. You don't want to constantly ask, "How am I doing?" "Was this okay?" "Did I do a good job with this?" because you'll come across as insecure and needy. I've had that kind of direct report and I can tell you it's exhausting. After a while, you tune them out—and that's exactly what you don't want to happen. Don't be a pain in the ass. Talk with your manager about how often to meet for their input on your work and progress.

Here's another factor to consider. Managers dislike giving feedback, especially constructive criticism. In general, not only do they find it difficult, but they generally suck at it. So, you may need to manage your manager. Don't wait until they come forward with feedback or you may be waiting forever, and that's way too late. In the meantime, you could be put on probation or even get a pink slip. (Ever wonder why it's called "pink"?) Be proactive, even if you have an inkling that some of the feedback may be negative. Bottom line is you need all the feedback—the good, the bad, and the ugly—in order to grow professionally and avoid future landmines. You need to be specific to get the precise type of feedback that will be helpful. Again, this is on you.

Here's a sample conversation:

You: I want to know how I'm doing with the current project I'm working on. In your opinion, what's going right and what needs improvement?

Your boss: I think the project is going okay.

You: Can you be more specific? Where do you think I'm doing a good job?

Your boss: I think it's all pretty good.

You: [*Frustrated as hell at this point and desperately wanting to take the good feedback you just received and end this painful discussion.*] For example, am I managing the client well? I know there was some tension in the relationship.

Your boss: Well, now that you mention it, the client has been unhappy with the lack of progress.

You: Did they say specifically what they felt unhappy about?

Your boss: They expected the project to be completed by now.

You: Yes, I understand. There were several hiccups that pushed out the timeline.

Your boss: I know, but the client needs to be informed when there are changes. I think you need to communicate more often and keep them in the loop.

You: How do you suggest I do that?

Your boss: Schedule weekly calls with leadership and send them regular updates via email.

You: Thank you so much for this feedback. This will help me manage the client going forward.

I think you get the idea, right? I know it's like pulling teeth but sometimes you need to draw constructive criticism out of reluctant managers.

What's important is that you drill down to the specifics without pissing them off or getting defensive yourself. Reassure your boss that this information will be useful and will keep the project on track for success. Make it all about the work and not about you, if possible. With practice, this will become easier for both of you.

Sometimes you may be caught off guard by a bad review, especially if you haven't had regular meetings with your boss to discuss this stuff openly. Even thinking about the prospect of getting hit with negative feedback, I can feel myself flush and my heart rate accelerate, and I'm just writing about this, not living it. When confronted with direct criticism, it's challenging to remain calm and receptive. Here are some things you can do when someone isn't satisfied with your work or behavior or both:

- Try your best to stay grounded. (See Part Three of this book for practices that can help with this.)

- Repeat what you heard to ensure you understood: "So, let me be clear. What I hear you saying is..."

- Ask for an example so that you can better understand the feedback.

- Ask for their thoughts on how to improve.

- Thank them for the honest feedback.

- Create a plan to turn it around. Share it with your manager, if appropriate.

- Hold yourself accountable for improving.

- Continue to meet with your manager and emphasize the ways you are working on the issue and following up on their suggestions.

Note to the wise: asking for feedback shows you are willing to do what it takes to produce good work and keep your job, maybe even get promoted. There's no age limit here.

Cultivate Your Growth Mindset

ONE QUESTION I like to ask myself at the end of each day is, "What's one new thing I've learned today?" And every day there's something. Not long ago, I attended a lecture by presidential historian Jon Meacham and learned so much about history that I wondered what the hell I had been doing in US history classes in high school and college! But the point here is that I learned a lot by going to the lecture.

I regularly go to events like this because I'm naturally curious and open to exposing myself to information and ideas that stimulate my thinking and expand my worldview. That's what a growth mindset is all about. And that mindset doesn't need to change over time. Your brain can always absorb new things as long as you keep it open. I remember my mother at ninety-five watching CNN for most of the day and holding her own in any conversation about politics and current events. Her curiosity and growth mindset never shut down.

Each week I interview a different amazing woman on my *Badass Women at Any Age* podcast and soak up all the wisdom and courage from my guests on topics such as leadership, owning your power, finding your passion, reinventing yourself, and more. I learn from their inspiring stories and it reminds me to be more present and mindful of my own journey. I learn a ton from other podcasts about science, history, our planet, politics, and music. What a wonderful world we live in today. There's so much information out there to take in and it's so accessible.

Asking yourself what you've learned each day increases your awareness about how much there is yet to soak up, on your own and from others. Because every day we're on this planet, there's so much to discover. And when we're open to expanding our horizons, whether by reading, taking courses, going to lectures, listening to podcasts, watching movies or TV, or speaking with others, we feed our brains. And feeding our brains is super-important as we age. So, maybe another question you should ask yourself each day is how you fed your brain. What did you *do* to learn something new?

One commonly held assumption is that as we age, we become more fixed in our mindset and therefore more likely to have strong, inflexible opinions. Mind you, you can have a fixed mindset at any age, which is characterized by a hesitancy to accept risk as well as a lack of openness to learning. I'm sure you know people, who may or may not be your age, who refuse to hear any opinions other than their own. That's a fixed mindset. For me, talking to people like this is frustrating as hell, until I recall that I sometimes get stuck in my own bubble too. There's always something to learn from others—even if it's that you don't want to continue the conversation because they annoy the crap out of you.

Regardless of age, people with a fixed mindset often feel helpless in the face of challenges, prone to accepting obstacles as insurmountable. I probably don't need to tell you that this type of mindset does not bode well for you if you're at a vulnerable age. A fixed mindset will enforce your belief that you're a victim who's unable to positively affect your future.

Now more than ever it's critical to demonstrate the growth-mindset characteristics of flexibility, resilience, and excitement about the opportunity to learn new skills. In a growth mindset, you believe that your most basic abilities can be further developed through dedication and hard work, that your intellect and talent are just the baselines from which to expand your knowledge and skills. Every day of your life is a new starting point. This mindset creates a love of learning and a positive attitude, which are essential for an active life and thriving career.

What does this look like in the workplace? One way to demonstrate your growth mindset is to clearly state your opinion in meetings without automatically disregarding ideas from your colleagues. It's easy to be blinded by how great we think our ideas are to the point that we tune others out. We're so convinced we're right that we see no other acceptable option on the table. This is dangerous territory. Sure, I want to encourage you to state your opinion with confidence, but if you don't listen to others who may have valuable input, your platform will be vulnerable to naysayers and critics.

Take advantage of every training opportunity that your company offers, especially courses to improve your tech skills. One woman I spoke with on this subject said, "Don't put your head in the sand and think that nobody's going to care if you don't know how to use Excel. If you're in a big company, they train you how to do this stuff. So, you have to show that you're in it to win it. That you're a team player, that things are changing, and that you're right there. Just because you're older and have been there longer doesn't mean that you can't pick up some of the new skills that everybody else has to pick up."

What courses are relevant to expand your skill set at work? If your company doesn't offer any type of instruction, request training or reimbursement for courses to learn new skills pertinent to your job and take some courses on your own. Show them you're still in the game. Ask your manager for suggestions or proactively research courses to improve certain skills or expand your professional toolkit.

If you have any doubt about your ability to learn new skills, your ageist assumptions may be hijacking your brain. Beware of interference from your evil inner critic again. She's always going to try to sabotage you under the guise of protecting you. Stay vigilant and on track.

Here's something new you can learn: neurologists and psychologists believe that the brain is elastic and supple during the years from age thirty-five to sixty-five and beyond. According to Jeffrey Kluger in *Time*, "the brain as it ages brings new cognitive systems online and cross-indexes existing ones in ways it never did before. You may not pack so much raw data into memory as you could when you were cramming for college finals, and your short term recall may not be what it was, but you manage information and parse meanings that were entirely beyond you when you were young." In other words, in midlife and later, you can maximize the ability to use all the information in your brain on an everyday, ongoing, second-to-second basis. An added benefit is that as the brain's flexibility improves with age, so does the temperament you bring to your work.

Here's some more information to take in. A long-term psychological study followed women for forty years and found that subjects scored highest in their inductive reasoning between their early forties and sixties. Their ability to objectively evaluate contradictory ideas peaked in their fifties and sixties. Yup, you read that right: fifties and sixties. Here's more proof that you still have great capacity to think creatively, solve problems, and manage data. The study also found that these women had an increased tolerance for ambiguity and improved ability to manage relationships, both of which are really important in the workplace. So, yes, your brain is still functioning on all cylinders even though you may need to give it a jump-start with caffeine some mornings.

Like listening to podcasts? You can absorb an abundance of the information that's out there at your leisure: driving to and from work, on road trips (my personal fave), in the gym, on walks or runs, doing chores around the house. Find podcasts that support your business skills and personal development or motivate you to play big. Ask your manager, colleagues, and friends for recommendations or simply search online. What new skills are you interested in, beyond work? Perhaps learning a new language or playing a musical instrument. After decades of not touching a piano, I'm taking lessons again. Try something new. With each new skill, you expand your brain's functionality.

While you're at the gym each day bemoaning the fact that your workout gets more and more boring and seemingly fruitless, remember that the brain, like a muscle, continues to develop especially when stimulated by physical exercise. So, you're doing double duty here. Your body and your brain benefit and you want both to be healthy.

Be a badass and exercise your brain. It ain't over until it's over. Be open to learning every day of your life and stay marketable and vibrant.

Build the Workplace Relationships That Count

AFTER COACHING WOMEN for more than a decade and conducting a boatload of research on the topic of women in the workplace, I can state with some authority that women desperately want to believe in meritocracy. We work hard and take pride in our work, and that's our comfort zone, that's what we can control. The idea of a meritocracy resonates with our sense of fairness, and we desperately want to believe it exists. You too may be holding on to a desire for fairness. *Isn't doing good work enough?* you ask. Simple answer: no.

No career is built in a vacuum, girlfriend. Sorry to hit you with this dose of reality, but I have to tell you that, at the end of the day, relationships are what will save you. You need a village of people behind you, especially those with influence and power. That's it. Ignore this advice at your peril. Because without relationships, especially when you're vulnerable, you're dead in the water, and this isn't a good time even to be treading water. Sure, doing good work is critical. I'm not discounting that. But that alone won't keep you afloat. You need all the lifesavers you can rustle up to champion you, support you, and encourage you to stay in the game.

Which relationships matter? They all matter to some degree. Pissing people off never does you any good, despite how angry you may feel for being treated like you're a nobody at times. Your reputation across the organization matters. Remember the *quality* of relationships is important, not the number of people in your network. But when choosing the best relationships to cultivate, you need to be strategic and prioritize. So, let's take a good look at how to approach this.

Identify the players

Start by identifying who has power and influence over your career. Use the diagram below from my book *The Politics of Promotion* to map this out.

Who is the decision maker? Is it your boss? Is it your boss's boss? Is there more than one decision maker? Put them in the center box below. Then fill in all the people who influence that decision maker. Look closely at who they have relationships with. Who do they pay attention to in meetings? Whose opinion seems to matter to them? Who do they hang with during lunch or after work? Intend to build visibility and credibility with all these people, along with the decision maker. You want them to be aware of the value you bring to the organization. Go back to your visibility plan for ideas on how to get on people's radar. (See "Be Visible," page 81.)

Create strong relationships

Create strong, mutually beneficial relationships with your colleagues. Plan to offer ongoing support to one another. (See the chapter on advocating for yourself and others.)

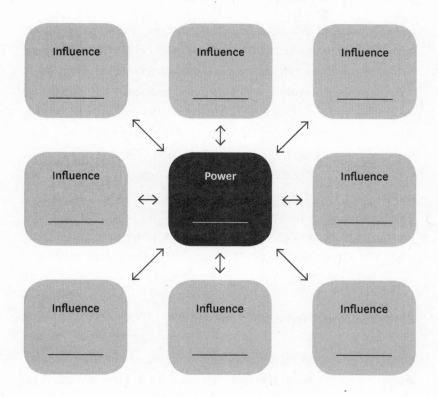

Who in your department can be a potential champion? What about people outside your department who work with you on different initiatives? Who's aware of the value of your work? Who's given you positive feedback in the past? List these people in your journal with the intention of nurturing these relationships. Let them know what you're doing. Find out what they're up to on a regular basis by meeting them for coffee or lunch. Don't count on a one-off meeting to have much impact. You want to grow these relationships over time. Can you help them in any way? Make it a win-win.

Who across the organization is a great source of information? You know, the people who always seem tuned into what's going on and what's coming down the pike, not the gossipers per se but people who pay attention and pick up on vibes that most of us miss. They can feed you information, make introductions on your behalf. They also have strong connections that can help you do your job better.

Let's say you're working on a project and you need IT's help to solve an issue with the software in order to complete your work. You've hounded them for weeks and they ignore you with every excuse under the sun: "I'm busy..." "I'll get to it this week...," but they never do. You're exasperated and realize your success depends on their timely delivery. What's going to move the needle here? Your best bet may be one of your allies who knows someone in IT who can help you push this through. And ta-da! All of a sudden, your project is a priority and it gets done in a week. Magic. The magic of relationships, actually.

Solicit support from your mentors

Mentors are important advisors and role models but they can also attest to your value and investment in your work. You want this type of support when things get tough or when you're seeking someone to speak up for you. This person can suggest that leadership consider you for a promotion, a raise, or a special project. This person can vouch for you when the company's considering layoffs and you're one of the vulnerable, more senior employees in the department.

Yes, like I said, you may need all the help you can get to avoid being shown the door because you're the oldest and perhaps the most highly compensated. The relationships that count can save your job, but you need to invest your time and energy in developing them. It's worth it because some day they may be your lifeline.

This may all sound manipulative and political to you, but remember you're fighting to maintain your status and secure your financial future. You must have people in your court who get what you bring to the table, believe in you, and stand up for you. And if these people have power and influence, all the better.

And don't burn bridges, for god's sake! Even if you're let go without cause and you're pissed (they say "downsizing" but you know the decision is ageist), keep in mind it's not your last job and you are going to want references. Dig deep to find some sense of diplomacy and hold back the vitriol you're dying to spit out. Instead call a friend outside work and vent. Write all the nasty comments in your journal, but don't shoot yourself in the foot, destroying the relationships you've developed by spewing your most bitter, angriest feelings at your former employer. As you're packing up your desk, people will likely come by and tempt you to share your feelings by telling you it's not fair that you've been let go, you're so terrific, and so on. It's so tempting to walk through that open door and bad-mouth your manager and the company. After all, these people seem to be on your side. But don't fall into the empathy trap here. I know, it may be challenging to resist, but remember that getting a job at this stage of your career is hard enough without sabotaging your future by telling your colleagues what a toxic place this is and you're happy to get the hell out. Take the high road, even though it sucks.

Remember that relationships encourage, support, promote, and advise you. Dedicate time each week to build and nurture the relationships that count.

Be Politically
Savvy

WHEN YOU BELIEVE in a meritocracy and keep your head down because you're focused on your work 100 percent of the time, you miss out on what's going on around you. You miss out on the workplace dynamics that can make or break your career. I'm not going to sugarcoat this by calling it by another name: you miss out on the politics. I know politics might make you cringe. You despise the political animals who seem to get what they want at work, despite their obvious self-serving manipulation. I researched how women feel about office politics for my book *The Politics of Promotion*. Sentiments ranged from "It's a waste of time" to "It's evil." Yup. That's what I've heard from hundreds of women.

But now it's time to grow up. It's time to accept reality before that reality bites you in the butt because you've got your head in the sand. Especially as you get older, you *need* to pay attention to office politics because you are increasingly vulnerable to being sidelined. Your survival depends on your political savvy. This means paying attention to how things get done, who wins and how they do so, and what it takes to successfully navigate your workplace. As we talked about in the previous chapter, it's about relationships.

You may need an attitude adjustment before you can get involved in what seems to you like a waste of time at best. I get it. Right about now you may be saying to yourself, *I don't care what Bonnie says. I'll never play the dirty game of politics.* Well, who said it has to be dirty? If that's what you're telling yourself, you absolutely need an attitude adjustment.

Stay with me on this. I want you to consider this scenario. You go out with some friends, let's say five or six, for a girls' night out. Excited and giddy to be together, you grab a big round table where you all can easily converse. Everyone's anxious to catch up, but for a few seconds before everyone sits, you stand around looking at one another and the table setup, assessing—perhaps unconsciously—who you want to sit next to, who you want to share your news and gossip with. Finally, somehow, it's negotiated and everyone takes a seat. Likely someone doesn't get to sit in her most preferred spot, but it's done. Some girl-friends get what they want and some don't. C'est la vie. Let's order drinks and let the rowdy conversation begin.

I'm sharing this scenario with you to point out that subtle politics go on even in our everyday situations. People have natural allegiances, favorites, and preferences, even within a circle of friends. And although everyone's out for a fun night, maybe they'd like to sit next to one friend over another for the next couple of hours. This, girl-friend, is politics. It is the dynamics between people. Who dominates the conversation? Who's getting the most attention? Who isn't? Who's everyone's favorite tonight? Who's trying too hard to gain favor? Is one friend hurt because she's talked over or left out of the conversation? Politics is not evil. It's not bad karma. It's how people relate to one another. It's real. In the workplace, it's no different. It's about people and relationships. Get my drift?

Here are some questions to answer to boost your political savviness:

- Who has power and influence over your career? Plan to build visibility and relationships with these people.

- How are decisions about promoting and firing made? Who decides? Make sure they know your value.

- What's the culture like? Is it collaborative, hierarchical, formal, casual, toxic, youthful, innovative, stifling, or prone to status quo thinking? What type of behavior is acceptable and approved? What isn't?

- How do you fit in this culture?

- How does the culture inform what you need to do to survive and thrive? What do you need to do, if anything, to better position yourself without compromising yourself?

- Is there evidence of gender bias? Ageism? Where? In which leaders? Who may throw you under the bus? Who could support you? Make sure you build a network of allies and champions who have influence.

- How does the culture affect your future viability and what can you do to adapt?

Write out a plan to position yourself for success. Use your political savvy skills as well as the suggestions from this book on advocating for yourself, creating a strategic network to support your career, and being visible and relevant. If you would benefit from some help with this, reach out to a mentor or hire a coach. Just don't sit on your ass like a victim waiting for doomsday.

Find a way to strengthen your relationship with your boss by letting them know how you can help them reach their objectives. What challenges are they facing? What's important to them right now? How can you become their advocate and help them gain more visibility for their work?

What does it take to get ahead or stay ahead? Don't make assumptions here, and don't state what you wish were true—for example, that your tenure could be based on your performance alone. Are certain relationships more relevant? Does a specific type of work carry more weight? What is the key to success? Most importantly for you, what does it take as an older woman to stay employed and be promoted? Get real and figure it out.

- Does the company support women or just pay lip service to gender equality?

- Are there any older women in senior leadership?

- How did they get promoted? Through relationships? Executive presence? How much did performance count?

Here are the key takeaways: Don't count on your great performance and hard work to advance your career or keep your job. Pay attention. Keep your eyes and ears open. Build visibility across the organization. Form strong relationships. Take control. Be proactive and learn to be savvy. Political savvy isn't evil. It's not a waste of time. It's necessary for your survival.

Learn to Say No

NO, NO, NO! Sometimes my inner voice screams at me to say no. The voice is loud and clear. *No, you really can't do this right now. Just say no. Say it.* But then my alter ego, Trudy, chimes in with her fear-based opinion: *If you don't do this, they will hold it against you forever. They won't like you. They'll spread nasty rumors about you and call you out as a stingy bitch.* And on and on. So, whose voice wins? If you guessed that I sometimes surrender my badass power and say yes even though I don't want to, you're right. I do. It depends on the ask and the person making the request, but I have to confess that my sweet, agreeable, eager-to-please self often steps forward and sabotages my badass efforts to stand up for myself. It's an ongoing struggle that many of us face. Now that we're over fifty and feeling especially vulnerable, it may cause us to say yes more, to try to be extra sweet and accommodating. But that doesn't help us in the end.

It's pretty obvious that an inability to say no when appropriate compromises you. When I back down and agree to something I don't want to do, I feel pretty shitty about myself and quickly question why the hell I didn't say no. *I know that it doesn't make sense to fly cross-country to do a full-day workshop in Buffalo, New York, for free.* I then try to rationalize it to make myself feel better. After I cave and agree to do it, I'll find reasons why it makes sense. *These women really need to learn how to advocate for themselves. I'll add value.* Or *I'll generate more business and sell books.* Or *I've always wanted to go to Buffalo in the dead of winter.* You know, telling myself stuff like this makes me feel better about agreeing to do something that just makes no sense or is against my best interests. But the point is that I'm aware of what I'm doing. I'm building a case against what I should have done in the first place, which is to definitively say no.

Why is saying no so difficult for us? Most of us, Boomer women especially, weren't raised to be badasses, to stand up for ourselves and what we believe in. Rather, we were brought up to keep the peace, maintain the status quo, please others, and sacrifice ourselves for the greater good. By the way, none of that's terrible, but we take it to the extreme and choose the path of least resistance to accomplish those things. Saying yes allows us to support the values we were taught as young girls.

Now we're all grown up. Supposedly, we've matured and learned some life lessons along the way. Yet I wonder how many of us have learned that saying yes when it compromises us makes no sense. How many of us repeatedly kick ourselves after giving in and agreeing to do something we don't want to do for a whole host of legitimate reasons, which at the end of the day never seem as important as pleasing someone else?

Saying yes to everyone all the time damages your reputation in the workplace. People will perceive you as the workplace doormat, and believe me, that won't secure your job. You'll be well liked because you never turn down requests, but you won't be respected and, as human nature dictates, people will take advantage of your willingness to please at every turn. Saying yes begets more requests. It starts to steamroll until it becomes much more challenging to turn people down, because they expect that you will always comply.

I caution my clients not to fall into what I call the "doer trap." The doer trap happens when you always say yes to requests from your colleagues. Will you help with this project? Can you teach me how to solve this problem? Will you clean the dishes in the kitchen? Will you plan the company picnic? Saying yes fills our to-do list with things that have no relevance to our job description. We get sucked in because we're agreeable and because, most likely, we do a good job at whatever we're asked to do.

The obvious danger here is that we spend way too much time on these tasks and have less time to focus on our actual job. Our work and our energy suffer. We get suckered into doing this stuff over and over again because to some degree people are genuinely grateful for our willingness to take an item off their to-do list and add it to ours. We are then complimented on a job well done. That makes us feel warm and fuzzy, good and appreciated, so then we're bamboozled into volunteering again ... when we could be out there closing more customer deals or doing more meaningful stuff. The praise and appreciation for this work is addictive. The problem is that it's busy work, not important work. At performance review time, none of this stuff matters. I mean, does planning the company picnic improve the bottom line or is taking care of it merely convenient to our colleagues?

I'm not telling you to say no to everything across the board. I'm simply warning you not to say yes to everything across the board. When someone approaches you with a request, slow down and do not respond immediately. Tell them you'll think about it and get back to them, and then actually do that. Think about it. Think about the source and the ask. How important is it that you say yes to this? Does saying yes position you better? Does the request come from a decision maker or influencer? Will it give you more visibility? Will you be able to leverage the experience somehow? Be strategic. Avoid requests from colleagues who just want to dump their work on you.

Sometimes the best response is to say no but you don't want to piss anyone off. An alternative is to offer to train someone else to do it so you can step away. It will take some time but then you'll be free of this activity in the future. Training and empowering others demonstrates your leadership skills.

Bottom line: don't be a sucker. Don't compromise yourself. Evaluate each request, put on your big-girl panties, and say you're sorry but what they're asking is not possible for you right now. That's badass.

Maintain and Grow Your External Network

WHEN I LOOK back on my career, I realize that I've gotten most of my jobs through recommendations from my network. In the beginning I didn't have professional relationships, but as I worked in different organizations, I stayed in touch with my former colleagues. Over time, these former colleagues opened doors for me and referred me for positions. These were people I'd worked with either directly or indirectly and they knew of my skills and experience. They had no problem making introductions for opportunities.

I was pretty beat up emotionally when I lost out on that VP promotion after working at the company for eight years. I knew I wanted to leave the organization and the male chauvinist bully I worked for. One day as I was catching up with my friend Cheryl, whom I had met at the company when we worked in the same region, I mentioned that I wanted to find another job. She had recently left for another opportunity, but we had supported each other personally and professionally through the highs and lows of working at the company. When we traveled for work and had to share a room, Cheryl and I always bunked together, covered for each other's sins at times, and thoroughly enjoyed each other's company. We became good friends and stayed close for years. I told her my newest tale of woe about losing out on the promotion. Cheryl informed me that there was an opening at the parent company where she now worked and she referred me for the job. I interviewed and got it. Thanks to Cheryl, I went from being passed over to president and CEO of a national company.

It turned out that, unbeknownst to me or the board, my new company was in dire financial straits. It didn't take me long to figure out that the previous CEO had cooked the books and the company was on the verge of collapse. It was a shit show and the leadership team I inherited had all played a part in the fiasco. It took a few months to convince the management of the parent company about the reality of the situation: that the business wasn't viable unless we made some drastic changes. We took a huge write-off ($40 million) and laid off more than two hundred people to pay for past mistakes. I designed a new plan for a consulting company with the twenty remaining employees, requested a package for myself, and left. I wiped my hands of that mess, but then I needed a job again.

I started doing some consulting work. Through my network again, I found out about a consulting gig working with a health-care tech start-up. A former colleague connected me with a guy who was starting a new business and needed some help finding a beta partner for his project. When I successfully identified and signed on a business partner for this, the consulting project turned into a full-time position as VP of sales, hiring, training, and managing a national sales team. And by the way, the beta company I signed was run by two former colleagues who knew and trusted me. Another win based on business connections.

Years later, after our major investor took control of that company, I needed a job again. I moved from Connecticut to Boston and reconnected with my former boss, Judy, who now held a leadership position at national company. She hired me for a regional sales director role, which quickly evolved into VP of sales, expanding and managing a nationwide salesforce again.

So, there you have it. My personal proof that building and maintaining an external network pays off. It's called your social capital, and it's worth every minute of your scarce time to nurture these relationships.

I recognize that there are many times in your career when you barely have time to brush your teeth let alone think about networking. You may not recognize its importance when you're happy and employed, but think of networking as your career insurance policy. Your network will provide opportunities in the future.

One of the most common mistakes we make is not being proactive or focused and intentional about networking. We don't consider it part of our work so we don't set aside time to do it, digging up a long list of excuses about why we don't have the time. Let's face it, most of those excuses are pretty lame. We rely on them to get us out of networking events because we're uncomfortable networking. Or we don't feel like putting ourselves out there to contact an old friend or former coworker. After a long day, we just want to go home and chill, put work out of mind.

But spending time nurturing your existing relationships and building new ones keeps you in the game. Consider it part of your job description now. Carve out dedicated time to network in person, online through sites like LinkedIn, or by email, text, and phone. Look for ways to add value to your network. Send an article that may be of interest and then schedule a follow-up call to discuss it. Reach out to a former colleague or manager at an industry event and suggest a coffee catch-up. When it's your intention to do it and it's on your calendar, you have a much better chance of following through.

Use your base network to connect you with people in different organizations and industries who have similar interests or backgrounds. You can easily search their networks on LinkedIn and request connections from their contacts. Or research different LinkedIn groups in your industry or general professional women's groups and start discussions. Attend outside networking events and lectures. These events can be industry specific or industry and gender specific, such as conferences for women in STEM, banking, insurance, or health care. It's a great way to build your network through common interests.

I've spoken with many women who haven't touched base with their contacts for years and feel embarrassed to reach out after the lapse in communication. But it's never too late to reignite relationships with former colleagues, college and graduate school alumni, and friends. Do this even if you're not looking for a new job. You never know when your connections will be helpful. You never know what information you'll pick up about the industry and what's happening in other companies similar to yours. Think of ways you can add value to your colleagues by finding articles, books, or podcasts that may be relevant or refer back to some interests you had in common.

I was coaching a client about reigniting her network and we discussed one easily overlooked benefit. When you're marginalized and undervalued at work, you may feel pretty crappy about yourself. It's hard not to. It brings you down, and you lose touch with how valuable you are. How wonderful it is to connect with former colleagues who have experienced working with you and appreciate your talent and expertise! It helps balance the negativity you experience at work and reminds you of what you've accomplished.

Bottom line: you never know when you'll need your network to help you find a new opportunity. Nurture what you have and look to expand your connections. This level of focus on your networking is badass and powerful.

Dress
the Part

TRUE CONFESSION TIME. When I worked in corporate companies, I spent a ton of money on my wardrobe. In my closet were Armani and Donna Karan suits, tailored to perfection for my petite frame, and high, high heels. (They weren't called stilettos then, maybe because the heel, although high, was thicker than the Louboutins today.) I considered the investment in my business attire to be a necessity of sorts. Maybe I was justifying my vanity, but I don't think so. I wanted to dress the part and look professional and powerful.

Here's the challenge with dressing the part when you're fifty-plus. You want to avoid looking old and frumpy at all costs. I mean, why would you draw more attention to your age by wearing baggy, matronly clothes with no shape or style? A professional look is tailored and neat. At the same time, you want to avoid looking like you're trying too hard to look young, with ripped jeans on casual Fridays or tops that show too much cleavage. It's a conundrum.

Our bodies are changing and the contents have shifted. Despite our best efforts to fight the love handles, we seem to grow thicker in the middle post-menopause. The wardrobe that worked at twenty, thirty, and maybe even forty doesn't work so well anymore; it could make you stand out like you're stuck in the dark ages (the '80s or

'90s?). Your appearance matters. It matters a lot if you want to stay in the game and position yourself as relevant and with it.

So, what's the best way to look powerful, hip, and professional in the workplace today? What's the best way to balance looking chic yet mature and experienced? Your appearance influences the way others perceive you and, most importantly, it affects your self-confidence and the way you carry yourself.

Scarlett DeBease, an image consultant, helps women create the right brand to fit their profile. She has several practical and useful recommendations for professional women over fifty. First of all, know what colors suit you best and then buy clothes only in those colors. She also suggests avoiding an all-black wardrobe because black can make you disappear and, god forbid, you don't want to be invisible. Wearing all black suggests you do not want to be seen and lack confidence. That being said, you can wear black, but accessorize with fabulous jewelry or a great big scarf to let everyone know you're not hiding.

Should you wear hosiery? One woman I interviewed shared with me that her younger female colleagues always commented on the fact that she wore pantyhose and made fun of her for it. DeBease recommends Donna Karan's The Nudes Pantyhose, if you feel the need to wear hosiery but don't want it to be obvious. Hosiery, except opaque tights, apparently makes you look old and out of touch these days.

Avoid being too trendy, but don't be afraid to experiment. DeBease encourages women to try different stores to avoid getting stuck in a rut. She notes that lots of women go to certain stores because the clothes fit, even though they don't like how they look and feel. Personally, I used to love going clothes shopping and now I hate it. Maybe I'd like it better if I had a personal shopper like the one I used to have at my favorite clothing store in Connecticut. She called me when a great outfit arrived in my size. When I was in town, I'd zip over and try it on, along with other clothes she tried to convince me I couldn't live without. But today I find the whole process overwhelming. I invest in online stylist services like Stitch Fix to find clothes for me, especially clothes that I ordinarily wouldn't try on my own. Stitch Fix replaced the role my daughter Abby played for me; when we shopped together, she used to pull things off the rack that I wouldn't have considered. Shopping with her was great, and I experimented with her guidance. It was part of the whole fun experience. However, with work clothes, you don't want to push yourself so far out of your comfort zone that you're self-conscious. Feeling confident in your body and clothes is important. Try being a little sassy, one outfit or maybe one pair of shoes at a time.

As for makeup, a lot of women tend to wear makeup the same way year after year, decade after decade, according to DeBease: "It's really important, in my opinion, every five years or so to get your makeup done. Get a new look because it can be very aging if you do your makeup the same way all the time. And less makeup is better as you get older." I'm usually bombarded with ads that promote makeup for older women, like lipstick that doesn't feather. I've never tried any of it, but it could be worth a shot, I suppose. You can find great videos and advice online about what type of makeup works best for women over fifty. I've learned a lot from some of these tutorials. Also, I sometimes take advantage when a department store or MAC offers to do my makeup, and I often end up buying their products (I guess that's the point), even though I can never replicate their results. I give myself an A for trying. You'd think I'd get better at applying it after all these years of practice.

Your hairstyle also has to be updated every few years, otherwise you can look stuck in the past. I'm not so daring here. A few years ago I contemplated cutting my hair short, but that fantasy was short-lived. I admit I hold an ageist bias that older women shouldn't have long hair, probably because when I was growing up, my mother and all her friends had short hair. Anyway, when I was considering short hair for a minute, I went to a wig store with my sister-in-law and tried on short-haired wigs, in part to prove to her that I'm not a short-hair person. She agreed. That was that.

At the end of the day, you decide what image you want to project and what makes you feel comfortable and confident. You can't control the changes in your body as you age, but you can control your image. Invest in your appearance. It needs to be part of your plan to stay marketable. It helps you on several different levels. When you feel good about yourself, you interact with others in a more self-assured manner. When your wardrobe is current and appropriate, you correct the misconceptions of your colleagues that you are "over the hill" and ready to be pushed out the door. You look professional and committed to staying in the game.

Respond to Ageist Comments without Getting Fired

KAREN SHARED SOME of the subtle jokes she heard from younger employees: "With the kids I'd worked with for a while, it was almost like a gentle teasing, which I got and I could laugh about. If somebody mentioned Abe Lincoln, the comment would be, 'Oh yeah, Karen. You went to school with him, right?' So, that's the ha-ha. I can laugh at a joke, but you think, *Ugh, it's just another thing. It's one other aspect of being old and a woman in that environment.*"

Every day women over fifty hear ageist, sexist comments. They may not be directed at them specifically, but they still sting. "Oh my god, she's over sixty. That's so old." "Oh my god, she's a dinosaur. She's aging out." Or "She's too old to change. She's an old thinker." One woman I interviewed told me that when she mentioned to a colleague that she was taking off work to get a root canal, the comment back was, "Oh, that's an old-person thing." Really? We can't even talk about our root canals without the fear of being labeled as old? Come on, my kids have had root canals.

A senior member of a legal team for a global company shared with me that she's often referred to as being "such a mom." Whether or not she's a mom, the ageist comment pigeonholes her into a role that has everything to do with her age and nothing to do with her function at work. Or she'll be the target of subtle jokes about some old music: "I'm sure you know that oldie, right?" The younger employees mock her with demeaning comments like, "Oh, look at you on Snapchat!" as if some unwritten rule states that Snapchat can be used only by people under thirty. Is there a politically correct comeback for a comment like that? I can certainly think of a few that aren't PC, but I'll keep them to myself. You can use your imagination to fill in the blanks.

The underlying message of these wisecracks is that being old isn't respected or valued at work, and it can be both a joke and a liability. Consider this: rarely are comments and jokes with racial, religious, or sexual overtones tolerated in today's workplace, but awareness of and sensitivity to ageism aren't on par with that of other discriminatory behaviors. And when sexism intersects with ageism, it feels like a real slap in the face. Quite simply put, older men aren't subjected to the same derogatory comments about aging as older women are.

So, how do you respond to such comments? You have a choice: you can let them go and just laugh along or you can let people know how these comments make you feel. I highly recommend the second choice, depending on the situation.

Some of these comments are made in jest. And people don't realize their impact on you. They may not even be aware that they're ageist. Give them the benefit of the doubt, a dose of reality (gently), and let them know how you feel.

Here's the tricky part. You need to hold back from being equally snarky, however tempting a snark might be. When someone says you are "over the hill," you may feel like saying, *I have more wisdom and talent in my pinkie finger than you'll ever have. Since when are you the authority on my competence?* But remember that you don't want to piss everyone off or get fired. The goal isn't to match their hurtful statement with an equally caustic comment.

On the other hand, you don't have to give away your power by laughing along with whoever made the comments, or take it on the chin and walk away without addressing how crappy it made you feel. So, you have to balance how to own your power with being direct and assertive. Leave your sarcasm for your journal at home.

To tap into the best mindset to deliver a firm but respectful retort, first take a deep breath and let go of everything you're thinking that's pissing you off. An angry tone of voice won't help the situation. Be mindful and chuck it before you open your mouth. On the other hand, a cowering response is a surefire way to end up being treated like a doormat. So here's the thing. It's important to understand where you're at emotionally to maintain your power position and size up the situation before you rush to a response that may further ostracize you or cause your dismissal.

Let's size up the situation. First, who made the comment? What's your relationship with that person? Your response may differ depending on how much power and influence they have. Was it a colleague or a supervisor? Second, where was the comment made? Was it directed at you? Was it said in jest to a larger group? When a colleague directs the comment to you, it's appropriate to respond directly. If it's made in a group setting, it's advisable to speak to the person one-on-one afterward.

The best approach if your colleague made the remark lightly is to acknowledge the comment, let them know how you felt about it, and then, if possible, reframe it positively to demonstrate your badass power. For example, if someone derogatorily refers to you as a "mother" or "grandma," don't immediately launch a counterattack. Address the comment and let them know how you feel about it. By acknowledging what was said, you're letting them know it's not acceptable.

You might respond with something like, "You know, I feel very fortunate to be a mother/grandmother. It's helped me in so many ways to be better at my work. My experience raising children has given me the wisdom and experience to be a better employee and offer tremendous value here."

I love Nancy Pelosi's thoughts on this topic: "Being a mom, what are you? You're a diplomat in interpersonal relationships. You're a chef. You're a chauffeur. You're a problem solver. You're a nurse. You're a health-care provider. You have so much, and that's just with the children, not to mention the other aspects of family." Pelosi recognizes that motherhood made her much more efficient and valuable to her work, and you can't find a more powerful role model than her.

And what if you're not a mother and grandmother? Does it piss you off when people assume that because you're a woman, you must have children? We are women after all. Isn't that what our purpose is? Well, not necessarily and that assumption reeks of sexism. And if they call you a grandmother, it's ageist as well, and meant to be demeaning. In that case, I'd acknowledge the comment by saying, "I get that you think I'm a mother/grandmother, but I have chosen a different path and I feel your comment is insensitive." Wow. Right on. I think they'll get your message.

What if a coworker makes an ageist wisecrack that you must've been friends with Abe Lincoln, as Karen experienced, or something similar? Again, you may want to remain silent or counter with a nasty remark, but it's wiser to demonstrate your maturity with a better comeback. "Ha! I certainly wasn't around then. But you know, I'm very proud of my years of experience. My experience enables me to bring both wisdom and value to my work and to this company every day." A response like that subtly acknowledges the ageism and places you in a strong position, one where you own the power of your age and history. You're not putting people down, although your inner child may be screaming to do so. You're not apologizing for your age either. You're standing in your power and demonstrating your maturity—exactly what you deliver every day. Don't let them forget it and don't *you* forget it.

How do you talk to your boss about ageism and sexism?

Discussing ageism and sexism with your boss or anyone else in a position of authority is gnarly, especially if they are treating you unfairly. You want to be professional yet let them know that their comment is inappropriate. And certainly, the tone and content of this conversation will depend on how strong your relationship is with your boss. If talking to your boss is impossible because of their toxic behavior or if there is an ongoing pattern of ageist comments and actions, I recommend first speaking with an HR person. But if you feel that your boss is reasonable and perhaps unaware that their remarks and/or behaviors are biased, a straightforward conversation is a good place to start.

Here the same approach is advised. Acknowledge the comment, and let them know how you feel about it. Say it like it is. However, avoid starting your discussion with "You said this" or "You did that." Those fighting words will immediately put them on the defensive. When you're in an attack mode, people shut down and can't hear a word you're saying. Try something like, "I felt it was inappropriate when you made the remark about older women. I found it offensive and it made me feel uncomfortable." If they aren't aware of their ageist comments, you're giving them the benefit of the doubt and helping them by pointing out their bias.

Keep in mind that making ageist jokes is so common in our culture that many people have no idea that they're offending anyone. But when you let them know how you feel, you're also putting them on notice. Ageism is not acceptable and shouldn't be tolerated, and you certainly do not tolerate it. Believe me, although you may be challenged by raising the topic, this conversation is nevertheless critical. Be direct, be tactful, and sister, show them you are no pushover.

If you feel your boss discriminated against you by not promoting you or not offering you opportunities or perks that younger workers receive, if ageist comments persist or are not made in jest—such as telling you outright that you're too old and need to move on—then take a more strategic approach, including consulting with an employment lawyer and filing a complaint with HR.

Know
Your Rights

J OANNE WAS HIRED as a pre-holiday salesperson for a trendy apparel shop for women. At fifty-two, she was excited about restarting her career after raising two children. To Joanne, the company felt like the kind of place where she could incorporate the skills she had formerly learned as an art director. She told her manager from the get-go that she wanted to move up, saying, "I love it here. This is the career of my future."

Joanne's enthusiasm was dampened right away, however. They sidelined her, assigning her to the fitting room in the back of the store. Several managerial positions opened up. Joanne was passed over for them all. But about six months into the job, when an assistant manager position became available, Joanne asked once again if she could apply. That's when Joanne's thirty-four-year-old manager said, "Let's talk," and took her outside the store, down to the dirty mall basement, where they sat on a wooden pallet to discuss her situation. Joanne was then told, "Listen, you are just too old for this company. Look around you. Everyone's young. Even the district managers are young. You're not going to have the stamina or the energy for this job. You're just too old." Ouch! Talk about a slap in the face.

Upset by the confrontation with her boss, Joanne called the company hotline to report the exchange, and that's when things got really ugly for her. She was transferred to two other stores, both hours away from her home. The reason they gave for these moves was that these locations had an older demographic.

Joanne's formal complaint must have put the company on notice, as she was finally given the promotion to assistant apparel manager, but it was an empty gesture. She had only the title, none of the responsibilities of that job. The company insisted she complete a special training program that required her to do ten closings and ten openings consecutively to train for the new position. That was a bogus requirement to make things tough for Joanne and she knew it, but she was happy for the promotion and still wanted to prove herself. She worked until one in the morning most nights to close the store and was up before dawn to make the long commute to do the open.

After just ten days into this job, she was told she was the worst assistant apparel manager they ever had: "You're too slow. You don't have the stamina or energy for the job. You don't have the pace that the other managers have." Joanne was devastated. Was she being set up? Most likely. It was pretty obvious that the company wanted her to leave on her own accord. What they didn't understand, however, was the strength of Joanne's ambition and desire to work. She wasn't going to quit.

Joanne instinctively knew what to do. She made formal complaints on the hotline. She started making copies of her schedule and documenting all conversations. Yet it wasn't until after she was fired from one of the two stores for some bullshit reason that she really pulled herself together and went to battle. She logged a complaint with her state's equal employment opportunity commission, and when she didn't hear back from them, she hired an employment attorney. Her case was eventually settled.

I'm telling you Joanne's story because it offers an important lesson. She was blatantly mistreated. Her managers, obviously never trained about employee discrimination, just blurted out their ageist agenda without any filter. They also demonstrated a clear case of poor judgment and lack of managerial skills. But Joanne, determined to keep her job, fought back. And after she was unfairly terminated, she brought her battle all the way to court. It took a large dose of stamina, courage, and persistence. Joanne chose to fight the legal battle. It's one option, and not necessarily for everyone.

What's the proper way to file a complaint?

My goal here is to inform you about how to protect yourself in a situation where you're being discriminated against, so I reached out for some legal advice. Heads up: a lot of really important information follows. Don't zone out on me here.

According to Davida Perry, a New York–based employment attorney, when you experience age discrimination, you should consult with an attorney to better understand your rights. Next, go to human resources and file a complaint. Make the agenda for the meeting clear: "I want to discuss the age discrimination that I am experiencing [with my boss, a coworker, or in my department]."

Describe the discriminatory comments or behavior without any fluff. Be direct. Be clear. Let HR know that you are aware that this is illegal activity. (Here's where a consultation with an attorney will help prepare you.) You might add whether you have already spoken to the person or persons involved and what the nature of that conversation was. Ask for acknowledgment that this is discriminatory and what the follow-up will be. In other words, hold HR accountable.

After the meeting, put something in writing, even a simple confirmatory email after the meeting. Put in the subject line: "Follow-up to our [enter the date] meeting." Here's an example of content for the body of the email:

Thank you for meeting with me on [date] about my concerns about age discrimination. As I mentioned in our meeting, I have experienced ongoing discrimination in my department. My manager, [name], has repeatedly told me I'm too old and has redistributed my work without cause. On several occasions, he has made demeaning comments about me in front of the team. Last week, he made fun of me and asked me in a group meeting when I was going to retire. You suggested that the next course of action would be that a representative from HR would meet with him and advise him of the consequences if he continues this action. We agreed to meet again in one month to follow up.

Use this example as a template. In your email, state what was covered in the meeting and any agreed-upon actions. It is critical that your meeting be recorded somewhere so the company cannot come back later and say, "Yeah, she came in and was talking about the fact that people are mean to her. Here are my notes and I wrote down everything she said." Hell no! That's not what was discussed! Don't fall into that trap. Write the follow-up email stating the meeting was about age discrimination, as Perry suggests. Get that on the record.

Letting HR and/or a senior leader know what's going on will empower you to pull yourself out of the victim mentality. Your documentation and complaint at the company level may not go anywhere legally, but you've taken action, stood up for yourself. Even if your actions don't protect you from getting pushed out the door, they can help with a settlement if you're handed a pink slip. And you always have the option of fighting the age discrimination.

Attorney Laurie Berke-Weiss suggests, "You want to be able to send the message in the most effective way possible if you believe that you're being targeted due to your age, that 'I'm on to you. I wasn't born yesterday.'" Berke-Weiss goes on to say, "If they think you're going to be a pushover and they're going to find a reason to get rid of you, you're telling them in so many words, 'We all know what this is really about.'"

Both Perry and Berke-Weiss recommend you talk to a lawyer at the first hint that you're being targeted. Find out what your rights are, even if you just have one consultation. Learn the ins and outs of building a case and what you should document going forward. Don't go it alone. Putting your head down and thinking it will all just go away and you can ride it out isn't an effective strategy. It is inviting the company to step all over you.

Isn't there a law against this?

Is there a law against ageism in the workplace? You bet there is, and it's important to know the law as well as the limitations of it, not only to protect yourself but to prove discriminatory actions. The reality is that the law, as it stands today, does not do much to protect older workers, especially women who face the dangerous combo of ageism and sexism. Congress enacted the Age Discrimination in Employment Act (ADEA) in 1967 to "promote employment of older persons based on their ability rather than age; to prohibit arbitrary age discrimination in employment." The ADEA prohibits age discrimination in hiring, firing, compensation, benefits, and any other aspect of employment. The law, however, hasn't fulfilled its promise. It's weak and ineffective.

According to Patricia Barnes, JD and author of *Overcoming Age Discrimination in Employment*, "there is no law in the United States prohibiting workplace bullying. So, it is not enough for older workers to show they were harassed in the workplace. To be actionable under the ADEA, workers must show the harassment was motivated by illegal age bias." And most importantly, you need to prove the harassment is beyond petty slights and annoyances; isolated incidents (unless extremely serious) do not rise to the level of illegality. You must show repetitive harassment over time and prove it is based solely on your age. This information is critical for you to understand when speaking with HR. To meet the requirements of federal law, you need to prove the pattern of comments or behavior is serious enough to be considered illegal.

There are many loopholes in the ADEA that companies take advantage of, which allow them to discriminate against anyone because of their age. They get away with pushing you out by calling your dismissal "downsizing," "reorganization," and a whole host of bullshit justifications. They find ways to get your birthdate or graduation date on your résumé when you apply for a job, and most disturbing of all is they often hire and promote based on how you look. And you'd better look young! Remember Lois Frankel's feedback after showing up for her interview with white hair?

Although the ADEA requires a high standard of proof for ageism, state laws can be more lenient in this area. You need to know what burden of proof is required in your state. For example, under federal law, which invokes the Equal Employment Opportunity Commission (EEOC), there is a severe or pervasive standard that needs to be followed. Before you file an EEOC complaint, you must demonstrate that you've attempted and failed to resolve the issues with your company. Following that, there are strict requirements to adhere to. You must file with the EEOC within 180 days of the discrimination. Then you have to wait sixty days before filing an ADEA lawsuit in federal court. This deadline may be extended, depending on your state law.

Where do you live and work? Since state employment laws may apply in your case, you need to research state law or, better yet, speak with a lawyer. According to Perry, in New York, for example, one discriminatory act can be sufficient. The law is broad, and you don't need to show a pattern. The standard in New York is to demonstrate that you're being treated worse because of your age or your gender or your sexual orientation.

According to California-based attorney Margaret Kreeger, you should start the process at the state level there too. She adds, "I do think there's an awful lot of information in California that would give plaintiffs of age discrimination claims a lot of background from which to proceed in the litigation. Or even to know that you should see an attorney before you sign anything when you're being put in one of those positions where you think it's based on age. And I think Californians know that very well—that you don't do anything without talking to an attorney."

Consider too, however, that suing your company is a long, arduous journey and although you believe your situation is unfair and you're right to sue their ass, the reality is that these lawsuits are challenging. Therefore, be very clear why you're considering this path. In Joanne's case, certainly she fought back because she was the target of abusive treatment. She wanted to be compensated for that. But she also took this on in hopes of building awareness about age discrimination against older women in the workplace. Her ultimate goal was to be able to change the stringent requirements of the law that make the burden of proof so difficult—so difficult that very few women, or men for that matter, fight back in court. She wanted some good to come out of all her suffering. But, that being said, going to battle with your former company is tough. Not only are you the David to their Goliath, but the process requires you to tell your story over and over again in public, and that can take a toll. Joanne shared with me that "suing these people is like adding insult to injury because you have to tell your story a million times. You have to deal with the other attorneys that are representing the company you're suing and they're awful. It's like pouring salt in the wound and you're wounded over again multiple times. You're told your suit has no value."

Margaret Kreeger believes that many people don't realize that suits involve a huge investment of time, energy, and money. Our only experience may be watching court cases play out in the movies or on TV, and therefore we think that everybody and their brother can just file a suit and there's no detriment to them. She says, "Even if you have gotten an attorney to take it on a contingency fee, it's a tremendous undertaking in terms of your emotional and physical well-being."

Joanne recommends that if you're getting involved in a legal battle, prepare yourself. Make sure you have family support. Make sure you have someone to talk to. You're going to need all that emotional support to deal with the digs on your character and competence. If there was ever a time to be a badass, it's now.

Negotiate the best deal you can

Say you have done your research and spoken to an attorney and your decision is to take a package and part ways with your company. Or you've been fired, you know it's based on your age, but you and your attorney have decided not to proceed with a lawsuit. Now you need to make sure you get the very best settlement. Believe me, it's easier to just pack up your desk and leave quietly, but you need to think about your future. Consider the fact that you may not be able to get another job easily or quickly because of your age. So, pull yourself together and fight for the best package you can get. Again, knowledge is power here, and getting your priorities straight is important.

Not only does negotiation on your own behalf require knowledge of your rights, it takes courage. Women almost universally suck at this. We haven't been socialized to negotiate well for our salaries when we're first offered jobs and we certainly don't do it for a package when we are let go. Isn't it easier to take the offer? No, it isn't. You'll regret not fighting for your best deal once you're out there trying to get another job.

So, where do you begin? Start by consciously deciding to make yourself your number one concern, maybe for the first time. Your financial future is on the line. You've worked for decades and sacrificed tons for the jobs you've held. And none of that was easy. For years, the company came first and now you have to let that go. You're not negotiating for the company any longer. You're negotiating for you. *You* are your primary concern. Be prepared to do what it takes to own your power.

Next, determine your priorities. Consider all the possibilities and then choose what is worth fighting for. You might start by researching. What kinds of things have other people negotiated for and received? This is true intelligence gathering because the company is not going to tell you. So, reach out to your networks in the organization and say, "I know this same kind of thing happened to Mary. Do you know what she got? Can I call her?" If possible, figure out what is within the realm of possibility. People may be reluctant to share, but what the hell! It's worth a try.

Here's some great advice from Carol Frohlinger, president of Negotiating Women, Inc. Ask yourself, *What's important to me? What do I want out of this?* Some people want the most money that they can possibly get, in a lump sum. Others might want years-of-service credit, to allow them to bridge the gap from wherever they are to retirement. Say you have a pension plan. Not too many companies do these days, but some people of a certain age have a defined benefits plan. There's usually a formula: X number of years of service and age equals you can retire with a pension. If that's the case for you, maybe you want to negotiate so that the formula works out in your favor, to cover the financial gap from where you are now to when you might have retired.

If you'll be looking for another job, you might negotiate for the kind of reference that the company will give when future employers call. That may include some kind of a press release. If you're at a very senior level, like general counsel, maybe you ask to work with them to draft it, so that your reputation is as protected as possible.

But as in any negotiation, there are trade-offs. For example, if you have five issues and they're all important to you, you have to prioritize them. You have to figure out which mean the most to you. And that depends on your goals.

Where are you in your career? If your goal is to find another job, you want to make sure you have enough money to bridge the gap until you're employed. Paula was sixty-five when she was booted out of a Silicon Valley start-up after just a year and a half. She had been hired by a young CEO and executive team who needed a lot of guidance on how to deal with their customers. The company had a bad reputation. Paula put in long hours fixing their system and educating the team. She did a fantastic job and everyone in the company loved her. But suddenly things shifted and she was told that she was no longer needed. Certainly, a nasty turn of events. It was a horrible feeling after all the time and effort she'd put in. But most disturbing was that they offered her only two weeks' severance.

Paula objected. "Two weeks. Are you kidding me?" So, she hired an attorney and sued them to get more. Documents went back and forth and Paula wrote detailed accounts of everything she had done for the company: "If they wanted to make a change and go in a different direction, I'm okay with that. But I need to be compensated properly for what I gave to that company." Money was her priority, and she was willing to fight for it. She also wanted the money to reflect her contribution. She knew her value. And as it happens, at the time of writing, Paula is still looking for another job and because of her age, she's finding it extremely difficult. Getting more than two weeks' severance was critical in the long run.

But keep in mind that severance is a benefit that companies give. It's not a right that anyone has. Davida Perry offers this advice: "To the extent that you can float an age issue to the company, you stand a better chance than just somebody who's been let go and wants more money." You really have to take some time and present the argument as a claim, as Paula did. The company must understand that if the issue is not resolved, there might be some legal action to follow. To competently address this issue, seek an attorney's advice.

If you're thinking about money, maybe you want to negotiate for stock options, depending on your company's stock purchase plan or your 401(k). Think about all the financial options.

Frohlinger adds that you might want to consider what else is important to you. For instance, you might want a retirement party. Or if you're concerned about leaving with dignity, ask to leave after closing on a Friday so you don't have to slink out the door in shame.

Think tactically and strategically about what's important, prioritize, and then ask. Again, there's so much value in an attorney's guidance here. I wouldn't put myself in the position of facing the big guns without knowing that I also have ammunition. Remember, David had a sling shot!

The biggest takeaway is that knowledge is power, sister. In order to stand in your badass power, the more you know, the better. Don't set yourself up to be pushed out of your company without a penny.

Be Strategic

ONE OF MY all-time favorite quotes from Yogi Berra is, "If you don't know where you are going, you might wind up someplace else." It makes perfect sense to me because I've always loved having a plan. A plan, however sketchy, makes me think that I know what I'm doing and can move forward with some degree of confidence.

When I decided to leave my corporate job and become a coach, I needed a solid plan. The goal was to get certified as a coach and start my own business. I had never ventured outside the comfort zone of having a salary and benefits, and I knew that I couldn't just jump out from under that security blanket to the cold, harsh business world without some direction. I had to understand the risk and minimize it wherever possible. There were tons of to-dos and I needed a way to hold myself accountable. That's where a strategic plan became important.

The first thing I did was investigate the profession of coaching. What was the potential income? Competition? What type of certification was available and what was the cost? Which programs were the best and which fit my budget and my work schedule? I knew I wanted training that was recognized by the International Coach Federation, which is the only accrediting body for coaching. I wanted that credibility. After some research, which included reaching out to coaches for advice, I found a certification course that fit all my needs.

I estimated my start-up costs. What resources did I currently have and what did I need? Could I prioritize those needs over time? I knew I should have a website at some point, but maybe not before I had some clients. I decided on the name for the business—Women's Success Coaching, which I have since updated to Bonnie Marcus Leadership—and bought the domain name.

I started coaching my colleagues and let former colleagues and direct reports know that I was available to help professional women advance their careers. People shared my information and referred me. I started blogging about helping women advocate for themselves and *Forbes* reached out to me to become a contributor. I wrote regularly and got the word out about my coaching services. I started getting booked to speak and do workshops. At first for free and then for a fee.

In the meantime, I changed my work status to 1099 (independent contracting) and, as my coaching business picked up, gradually decreased my employment hours from full-time to part-time, until I reached the point where I thought I could at least break even. Then I left my job and became a full-time entrepreneur.

Sounds so simple when I retell this story, but let me tell you, it wasn't. And it wasn't accomplished without some mistakes and mishaps. But what kept me on track when I'd sometimes stray off the road? What kept me going when my fears and self-doubt started to gnaw at my confidence? You got it. I had a strategic plan!

Having a goal is a good thing. But a goal without a strategic plan is pie-in-the-sky nonsense. That's like waiting for the universe to reward you just for the hell of it, when you don't have any skin in the game. A strategic plan to reach your goal gives you focus and intention, all positive vibes for staying connected to your ambition. Like a GPS, your strategy prevents you from straying off course and directs you forward by mapping out each turn, roundabout, obstacle, and potential detour. If I had only the goal of becoming a coach without a path to get there, I probably would have made more costly mistakes and it would have taken more time to transition from my full-time job.

You may push back and say, *Yes, but what if this? And what if that?* Or you may feel so negative about your future that you can't even think about it and so you're paralyzed with inaction. If that's the case, you are stuck. Admit it. Maybe the first move out of your comfort zone is gathering up enough confidence to identify a goal. Because that is the hardest part. Take baby steps and choose a small one. Maybe it's not world domination the first time out of the gate.

We fool ourselves by thinking that any goal we choose is carved in stone and can never be modified. That belief makes it a challenge to decide what we want without breaking into a sweat. We think, *OMG, do I really want to commit to this?* We get cold feet about the whole process. I know the feeling. As soon as we choose a goal, we immediately begin to doubt our ability to reach it and then sabotage ourselves before we take even one step toward it. But that's where the strategic plan comes in. Follow me on this. The plan shows you exactly what you need to do to accomplish what you want. Your goal is not a pipe dream anymore because you've defined the path as well as all the steps on the way. A plan is your best bet for making it happen.

What do you want for your future? What's your goal? Be specific and use SMART (specific, measurable, attainable, relevant, timely) goal guidelines to help you develop the plan. Maybe you need a financial plan to figure out how and when you can retire. Perhaps you want to plan your exit from your company to start a business on your own. All these initiatives require a strategy to be successful. Write this down! Here's an example.

> **Goal:** I want to transfer to a lateral job in another department within my company by the first quarter of next year.
>
> **Step 1:** Gather information. What's the company policy? Do I need to go through HR or my manager first? What's the culture and leadership like in the department I want to transfer to? Does it seem like a good fit and a good career opportunity? Who are the decision makers and influencers I'll need to involve?

Step 2: Discuss possible move with boss. Can I get their support? Create a plan with them about date of move, potential replacement, training of replacement, and so on.

Step 3: Connect with my network to see who can make introductions and open doors for me with a new potential manager.

Step 4: Solicit support from influencers, allies, and mentors.

Step 5: Meet with new manager to discuss the prospect of relocating. Use my value proposition to demonstrate how I will enhance their team. Identify if I need additional skills or experience for the position and plan out the steps I need to take to qualify if so.

Step 6: Identify a timeline for the transfer.

Step 7: Get buy-in from all parties.

Even better is to use a spreadsheet that lists each step in your strategic plan, a time frame, next steps, and follow-up.

ACTION	TIME FRAME	NEXT STEPS	FOLLOW-UP
Gather information	April		
Discuss possible move with boss	End of April		
Connect with network for introductions	May		
Solicit support from influencers, allies, mentors	May		
Meet with new manager to discuss prospect of relocating	June		
Identify a timeline for transfer; get buy-in from all parties	July		

Get the idea? This type of goal setting and planning is what being strategic is all about. But bear in mind, as you go along, the plan may change. You may have to add more steps or eliminate some. You may decide to scrap the whole damn thing and start over if you realize that it's not realistic and/or you no longer want this goal. That's okay too. But don't scrap the goal-setting process and the strategic mind-set altogether. Keep moving your life and career forward by revisiting your goals. Remember, you wind up somewhere else if you don't know where you're going.

Land a
New Job

MAUREEN HAD JUST turned fifty when she was laid off last year. She shared with me how extremely difficult it is as an older woman to even get an interview. A seasoned attorney, she's looking for a general counsel position. "I can't tell you how many times I've been told, 'You're overqualified. You're more firepower than we need. We're looking for someone more junior. We want someone to grow into the position. We want someone who's more dynamic or more the age group of the rest of employees.' I've lost out on just a ridiculous number of jobs over the last year to people who were significantly younger and clearly not experienced."

Here's the reality. Most likely her age, gender, and salary expectations affected her ability to get hired. I've heard this tale of woe from many women over fifty who are trying to find new positions after they've been let go. Let's be clear: the reality sucks. It ain't easy to find another comparable job at this age—but it's doable. You need to show that you're marketable, lead with your value, and position yourself as someone who can help a prospective employer reach their objectives.

Linda Descano, executive vice president at Red Havas, shared with me how at age fifty-five she successfully transitioned from an executive position in financial services to a new leadership role in the PR industry. First, wisely, she gave herself some time to decompress and work through her grief after she was let go. Initially, the notes she received from her former colleagues helped a lot. They reminded her that her value wasn't in her title. It came from her knowledge, experience, network, and her willingness to put those assets to work to support others. She embraced her continued value.

Linda recognized the importance of a routine, so she didn't lose herself to the addiction of daily soap operas. (Yes, it is so easy to get drawn into *General Hospital*. Linda resisted.) She instinctively knew that she had a new full-time job, and that was to find a new job. Linda woke up and worked out at the same time each morning. She took a spot at a coworking space so she had a place to go each day. She started working with an executive coach for a critical analysis of her skills, interests, and potential career directions, and she polished her résumé and LinkedIn profile to position herself well.

Next, Linda reached out to women in her network who were let go or decided to leave their company and who had transitioned to new positions. Their guidance was enormously helpful. But then, around six weeks after receiving notice, Linda shifted her networking efforts. She started organizing networking coffees focused on the future rather than on her displacement. It was through one of these networking coffees that she was introduced to a woman who immediately recognized Linda's talent and potential to add value to her PR firm. She set up an interview and Linda was hired.

Linda did a terrific job preparing for her employment search. She adds this bit of inspiration: "There is no age limit on reinvention. The key to successful reinvention is curiosity, being okay making mistakes and taking guidance from—or even working for—people much younger than you, learning new ways and unlearning old ways, resilience, and a can-do attitude."

Let's dig a bit deeper into what specific steps you can take to best position yourself.

First, does your résumé need an update? Make it as ageless as possible. Shorten it and focus on your last ten years of employment, remove college graduation dates and the like, revise any outdated terminology, and use powerful verbs, adverbs, and adjectives in your job summaries.

Quantify your results when possible. Here are some examples:

- I successfully led the team to produce timely results, which increased our bottom line by *25 percent* this past year.

- My innovative solutions resulted in a user-friendly, customer-focused product that increased revenue by $40,000 over the last two years.

- I effectively organized and coordinated teams across departments and motivated them to stay on track until project completion, beating all deadlines.

- I analyzed the problem and created a dynamic out-of-the-box solution that saved the project and led to more efficient processes going forward.

Tailor your résumé and cover letter to a specific job opening. For example, if you're applying for a project manager role, emphasize important achievements in this area and critical skills for this role—for example, team building, communication, motivation, technical expertise with the software, and so on. Make yourself appealing to a new company. Highlight that you are a team player, tech savvy, flexible, open-minded, willing to learn. Ask yourself what would be important to you if you were the hiring manager for this position. Include any recent training or conferences you've attended to show you are up-to-date in your profession.

Next, the interview: above all else, prep for it. Know your value proposition and how your work leads to positive business outcomes.

Give examples. This is a powerful way to position yourself to get another job. Let your potential employer know how you can help them reach their objectives. Research the organization or ask them: What are your goals for this year? What are some of your challenges? Once you know the answers, then you can position yourself to help, using your value proposition. For example, "I saw on your website that you have some ambitious goals around improving customer satisfaction and revenue. I can help you in this area. I have the unique ability to connect quickly with customers, build relationships of trust, and influence that has helped repair damaged relationships and upsell new business opportunities. In my last company, these strong relationships resulted in a 34 percent increase in customer satisfaction in one year and a 15 percent increase in sales from existing customers."

Your comfort level in an interview may be to simply regurgitate your résumé. Resist the temptation to do this. They already have your résumé, so if they agree to interview you, you don't need to recount twenty years of experience. Instead, talk about how you can help them move forward. Don't dwell on your history except to give concrete examples of achievements. Talk about the future and how you are the person to help them get the results they desire. Talk about how you took a new approach that paid off, or perhaps an example where you interacted with all levels of teams and let others take the lead in certain areas.

And don't be boring. Pace your energy throughout the interview. Actively listen so you can respond intelligently, and ask good questions based on your research about the company and market as well as what you hear them say in the interview. Also important is showing your enthusiasm for your work and the opportunity they're offering. I know that goes without saying, but when you get nervous and are focused on saying the right thing, this is easy to forget.

Here's some additional advice for the interview:

- Practice with a coach, trusted friend, or colleague.

- Research the company and industry and prepare a list of smart questions.

- Pay attention to your appearance. Go to the website to look at company photos. What seems to be the appropriate dress? Don't dress too formally or too casually, even if it appears to be a casual work environment. You want to look professional and serious.

- Overcome the assumption that you're overqualified or want too much money. If you're above the salary range posted or if the topic of overqualification comes up, let them know in the hiring process that you're prepared to take a pay cut.

- View all your interviews as lessons and debrief with yourself afterward. *Where can I improve? What went well?*

Finally, get active on social media. Show that you're engaged and knowledgeable about the industry. Write articles on LinkedIn, post articles on Facebook and Twitter, comment on articles that others write and on new ventures you see posted on LinkedIn. Relate these things to your own experience. If you go to a conference, share what you learned on social media. Find people who work at companies you're targeting for a job and then follow them on social media. If a senior manager at the company posts something online, comment on it to show your interest and support. This all goes to fight the stereotype that if you're older, you just want to relax and unwind with your grandchildren. That is not the kind of person a prospective employer wants. Actively network on social media to create leads for new jobs. Start with who you know: your network of former colleagues. Use LinkedIn to search companies and make connections as well as learn about industry events.

And the most important requirement for landing a job is to believe in your value and dismiss all the negative chatter in your head that you won't get a job, you're too old, you're overqualified. Yes, all that nonsense. Because that mindset more than anything else will sabotage your chances. And give it your all. Finding a new job is a full-time job.

Part Three

BE YOUR BADASS SELF

I was a badass kid. I was so confident and precocious that my constant desire to be in the spotlight may have made my parents proud, but it pissed off my older brother. I unconsciously upstaged him by simply being me. Here's a good example of badass Bonnie: my love for ballet started at four years old when I first took lessons, and it seemed so natural for me to take my ballet shoes with me everywhere and offer to dance. When I was six, I asked the band leader at my cousin's wedding to clear the dance floor so I could dance in front of the 125 guests. No kidding. If you're an older sibling, I'm sure you can empathize with my brother.

I'm not sure where my badass attitude came from but I do know this: it didn't last. It probably started to wane when I was in middle school. That's when I became very aware of my looks and whether or not I was attractive to boys. Although I had always wanted to be a good girl and tried to earn praise from my parents and teachers, pleasing and appealing to others was now my priority. The result? Any badass attitude was totally gone by high school. Over the course of my adult life and career, that mindset has emerged then retreated in cycles. Now I intentionally nurture my confidence and challenge myself to step up and play bigger: to be a badass.

I'm not going to make a sweeping statement here that all women over fifty have similar stories. But I do know from coaching and speaking to many women in this demographic about this topic that the story is familiar, despite our own unique histories. Whether or not you were a badass little girl, nurturing that attitude now and showing up at work and in the world as your authentic, powerful, talented, amazing self are essential.

They are essential because as we age, we don't exactly have the support of society and we certainly don't have support from the workplace. We've already discussed how this is true. Our age works against us, as does our gender, and we can't take this shit lying down. I, for one, am not ready to roll over and play dead because I've passed fifty and others may believe I'm over the hill. And I hope you won't either. You've got too much value to offer your company and society. That's why nurturing your inner badass is critical at this stage of your life and career.

Staying connected to your inner badass gives you the courage to advocate for yourself, speak up, stand up for what you know is right, and not back yourself into the shadows and out the door.

How do you nurture your inner badass? First of all, you need to take back control of your life and work by putting yourself front and center. In the following chapters, you'll find encouragement and support, as well as proven tools to help you step up your game with confidence. I know this may be challenging if you have always taken the back seat and lost yourself in the process. But now is your time to love yourself, find joy, and rediscover what you may have lost over the past couple of decades: that you're a smart woman who still has years of valuable contributions to make at work and in the world.

Katie Couric defines a badass woman as someone who "stands up for herself, is confident, and is not afraid to challenge the hierarchy, the patriarchy, or conventional thinking." That's what I'm talking about, girlfriend. Be proud. Stand tall. Be a badass.

Take Back
Control

'VE NEVER CONSIDERED myself a control freak, yet things beyond my control are the biggest sources of frustration for me. When things start going wonky with my iPhone or computer, it seriously stresses me out if I can't figure out how to fix it on my own. When the cable goes out and I'm psyched about watching the next episode of *Homeland* or catching up on the news of the day with Brian Williams, I'm pissed. Right now, I have a Netflix dilemma. In the living room it works fine, but in my bedroom it's in Spanish and I can't figure out how to change it back to English. I mean, how the hell did that happen out of the blue? It's out of control.

I know some people thrive on adrenaline highs, jumping from airplanes and pushing their physical limits. That isn't me. My astrologer would probably tell me that's because I'm a Taurus. But this I know: I feel most powerful when I have control of a situation, or at least when I think I do.

What's interesting to me is that when I feel I don't have control, I start to lose control. You know what I mean? My worst self shows up. I'm not rational. I become totally emotional and reactive, don't think straight. I'm not suggesting I throw things at the TV or punch my fist through the wall. Geez, I'm not that out of control. There's a spectrum here, and all in all I'm fairly level-headed. Once triggered, I do recover pretty quickly. How? My most rational self will jump back in, take control, and say, *What the hell do you think you're doing? Get yourself back on track*. But my fear of not having control is real, and let's face it, the aging process definitely provokes an uneasy sense of losing control.

Here's my truth: I don't want to hear anyone tell me that I'm too old to do anything that I still feel confident doing. I don't want anyone to make assumptions about me that limit my opportunities to be who I am or marginalize me or silence me because I'm aging. I want to control my body, my life, and my work for as long as I am capable.

If you're with me on this and hate the feeling that you're losing control of your life right now, let's look at the things you *can* control. Because there are a lot.

First, there's your body. Don't give me the bullshit excuse that menopause has hijacked your body and you'll never see your waist again or sleep through the night. Or that having children ruined your figure and you'll be lucky to ever fit into your skinny jeans again. With a little self-discipline, you can control your body by deciding not to abuse it. Cut back on or cut out alcohol, sugar, caffeine, and all the crap that makes you feel sluggish and unhealthy. Oh, this can be so hard some days when you're craving massive amounts of chocolate and can't wait to get home from work to unwind with a glass of wine. Even the promise of that glass of wine may be the only thing motivating you to push through some days at work. I get it. I've been there. But a glass of wine is different from devouring most of the bottle. Ah, sweet discipline. Where are you when I need you?

Personally, I can't stand the thought of going cold turkey and totally eliminating all this stuff, so my way of taking control of my health is by demonstrating discipline. And although I admit it can be tough, I feel better by exerting that control. I eat well most of the time, exercise, practice self-care, and try my best to honor my body. After all, it's the only one I've got and I want it to last.

What are some ways you can take control of your body? Make a plan, and write it in your journal. Then make it your intention to honor the plan. Each week, celebrate when you stick with your plan, and in a way that *does not* include undoing your achievements with binges of chocolate chip cookies. That goes without saying, I hope.

What are some other ways you can take control of your body? Write them down and honor them. Here are some examples.

I commit to honoring my body by:

- *Exercising _____ days a week. [You can also fill in what that exercise is, for example, walking, swimming, running, hiking, dancing...]*

- *Limiting my alcohol intake to one drink a week. [Okay, two on special occasions, but try not to create bogus special occasions just to have an extra drink. I know all the games, girlfriend.]*

- *Going to the doctor and dentist regularly for checkups. Monitoring my cholesterol, blood pressure, sugar, and so on. Getting eye exams, mammograms, pap smears. [It's true that none of this is fun, especially getting your teeth drilled or your breasts squeezed beyond your tolerance for pain. But remember you're taking control of your health and well-being here.]*

- *Booking a facial and massage at least once every two or three months. [Personally, I do facials once a month and it's such a glorious way to honor my body and take some control over the aging process. Don't tell me you can't afford it. Once you're cutting back on the wine, you'll be surprised how much money you have.]*

Next, you can control who you let into your life. Okay, you can't choose your family but you can certainly decide how to interact with them. Sometimes dysfunctional families take a toll on your self-esteem and health. If that's your situation, try your best not to get into the weeds and give yourself some distance from the toxicity as much as you can. For most of us, though, our families are a great source of encouragement and, hopefully, unconditional love. Don't hesitate to welcome that love into your life. That love can be your best support when times get tough.

Unlike family, you can choose your friends. Choose wisely. I prefer having a couple of very close girlfriends rather than a crowd, but you may be different. I don't share my most intimate thoughts with everyone. However, my girlfriends are always there for me and vice versa.

When it comes to romantic partners, you can control who you let into your life as well. I'm learning how to choose my lovers and partners carefully. Boy, I've made some lousy choices in the past, but I finally get who I am and what I want and need in a relationship. It's taken me a divorce and decades of heartbreaks and breakups. That awareness gives me control. Now I feel whole and happy to be living my life to the fullest, with or without a partner.

You control how and where you want to live. I've always chosen to live in beautiful places, usually by a river or ocean. It feeds my soul. A few years ago, after giving the opening keynote at a conference at University of California, Santa Barbara, I took someone's suggestion to go for brunch at the beach on the way back to Los Angeles, where I was staying with my daughter. I ordered myself a rather large Bloody Mary to celebrate my morning accomplishment and then I looked around. I said to myself, *Oh my god, this place is beautiful.* Mountains on one side, the ocean on the other. (If you've ever been to Santa Barbara, you know what I'm talking about.) At that moment, I took control of my life and made it my intention to move there. And within two months, I relocated across the country and settled in Santa Barbara, where I now live and celebrate my life every day.

Where's your happy place? You don't need to move to find it. Maybe it's a special beach or mountain hike or garden. Spend time there to just sit and take in the beauty. Breathe it in. Feel that sacred space in every cell of your body.

Most importantly, you control your attitude, which affects everything in your life and career. Your attitude can support your success or sabotage it. Again, it boils down to choices. You can choose:

- to look at problems as the end of the world or as an opportunity to grow and learn;

- to be a doormat or find ways to take back your power;

- to remain invisible or advocate for yourself;

- to be silent or to speak up, stand up for yourself, and let people know how you feel;

- to abuse your body or honor it;

- to stay in toxic relationships or let them go;

- to just coast along biding your time and risk being sidelined or embrace your ambition and talent, to do your best work each day; or

- to stop apologizing for your age or own it and love it.

Let's make a plan to take control of your life. Sounds daunting, but we'll take eensy baby steps. Respond to these statements in your journal:

- Here's how I'm taking control of who I let in my life.

- Here's how I'm taking control of my living situation.

- Here's how I'm taking control of my attitude.

Now, how do you accomplish taking back control at work? You need to dig deep and find your inner badass power and stand tall.

Taking control of your career is a choice. Choose to fight for your future. Decide not to lie down and be steamrolled. You deserve to be treated well and respected. If you're constantly passed over, dismissed, and disrespected, stand up for yourself. Talk to your manager. Talk to HR. Let people know how you feel. If work is really a source of stress or raising your blood pressure, move to another department or company. Don't be a victim. Follow all the advice in this book.

Remember, one of the most empowering things you can do is to find a way to take back control when you feel others controlling you. You have one life. Live it on your terms.

Get Out of Your Comfort Zone

AFTER DOWNING that large Bloody Mary post-keynote at UC Santa Barbara, I made the decision to move cross-country. I love making plans so I immediately put the wheels in motion with gusto. But what I quickly learned is that although planning is in my comfort zone, taking such a big leap... not so much.

The planning went smoothly. I was in heaven writing to-do lists and crossing items off each day, feeling so proud of myself for accomplishing stuff. Downsizing was a chore but it had a greater purpose. Donate books to the library, clothes and unnecessary or outdated stuff to Goodwill. It's truly amazing how much crap we collect that we have not used in years or don't remember having in the first place. Once you start downsizing, you suddenly notice all this stuff piled up everywhere, and there are tough choices to make about what to keep and what you can live without. It's overwhelming. At first every decision is monumental. *Do I really need two sets of dishes? Do I really want to pay to move two sets of dishes?* And then over time you just get numb and start tossing everything.

Dutifully obeying my to-do list, I got lost in the process and perhaps the excitement of a big change. But, oh my god, it was a big change, a really big change. I'm an East Coast gal and except for a short stint in Chicago for work, I'd lived there my whole life. I went to Connecticut College and grad school at NYU. So, I never really ventured outside my little northeastern bubble much until this move.

Somewhere along the way, as I was telling everyone of my pending relocation, anxiety set in. I started to realize that this was a huge break from my cozy bubble and it was scary as hell. My entire support system was in Connecticut: my brother, my friends, my dentist, my doctors, my chiropractor whom I trusted, my hairstylist whom I had been with for decades and loved. But as Yubing Zhang said in her TEDx Talk, "Life begins at the end of your comfort zone." And I had reached the end of mine.

Even before the physical move, I networked to find new work opportunities in California, to jump-start my business on the West Coast. I attended a couple of workshops in LA and Santa Barbara and found some like-minded women. Once settled in my new apartment, I joined Match.com and started dating. Yeah, talk about being out of your comfort zone. That was a trip. But I met new people and learned a lot about my new city. And even though I've been here for almost three years, I sometimes still feel uneasy and crave that snug-as-a-bug feeling of knowing my surroundings and having a supportive network of friends and resources. I'm becoming accustomed to the Californian culture, and I'm discovering new resources (yes, including a hairstylist I love and trust, thank god) and connecting with a wonderful group of friends. It's definitely not the East Coast, but it's growing on me. I guess, in part, because I'm creating a new comfort zone here and feeling energized by it. Every day is an exciting adventure.

Do you challenge yourself to step out of your comfort zone?

Although warm and welcoming, complacency can stop you from growing, learning, living your best life, and reaching your full potential. I know that may sound pretty trite, especially the "reaching your full potential" bit, but think about it. Once you become so complacent doing what you've always done, you're stuck. And I mean major-league stuck. Stuck in your sense of security and the status quo. Is that the way you want to live the rest of your life?

Let's imagine that you are very comfortable with your current job and in your company even though you aren't compensated fairly. What might be the consequences of that? You might be compromising yourself and sacrificing your financial viability for that comfort zone. An obvious consequence may be in your pocketbook, but being underpaid also gnaws at a person's self-esteem. You feel underappreciated and lose a connection to the value you offer a company. You may feel they're taking advantage of you, but your complacency holds you there.

Breaking out of your comfort zone, by the way, doesn't necessarily mean quitting, but it does mean willfully overcoming complacency.

Here's a sample break-out-of-your-comfort-zone plan:

Do your homework. In the example above, you could ask some of your trusted colleagues what others with a similar job description or grade level are paid. People may be reluctant to share this info but give it a try. Is your company currently posting jobs at the same level on its website? Check out if the salary range is comparable. Look at sites like GlassDoor.com for similar jobs in your industry and region.

Get ready to leap. Gather your information and get ready for a huge leap from your comfort zone, negotiating and advocating for yourself. Put on your big-girl panties and request an appointment with your manager or HR representative to review your salary. Decide before-hand what you want and are willing to take if offered. Are there extra perks you might accept in place of a dollar increase? More vacation time, a larger bonus, more stock options, more flexible time to work at home?

Make your case. Present the salary information you've researched. Beforehand, create a value proposition statement and list of recent accomplishments. Quantify your results as much as possible. For example, "My ability to build trust with customers has resulted in a 25 percent increase in new revenue in the past six months." If the company only approves salary reviews at year-end, ask for a commitment for the increase at that time.

Keep at it. If your ask is declined, don't let them off the hook. Request specific reasons for the denial and ask for a follow-up date to review.

Did I lose you? Are you so far out of your comfort zone that you can't imagine putting yourself in this situation? Negotiating on your own behalf is a new skill, and it demonstrates confidence and leadership. And what do you have to lose? They may say no, but I guarantee that your manager will have more respect for you sticking up for yourself and your work.

The outcome isn't as important as the action itself. Once you start building this new muscle, you can use it in other areas of your life, including relationships and personal and professional growth. For instance, take a course you've always wanted to do but have hesitated about because it was too scary, too big a leap.

Write a list of how you think you can stretch a bit.

You don't need to take a huge leap. Choose one area in which to stretch. Start with a changement or, if you feel bold, a grand jeté.

Life is short. You don't have forever. Staying in your comfort zone is boring, boring. If you never stretch yourself to learn new things or tackle new experiences, you grow old and stale fast. But stepping out of your comfort zone not only gives you confidence, it energizes you. You feel pretty damn good about yourself after the initial uneasiness, and you appear more youthful to others. If you're willing to get unstuck, I can guarantee you'll feel better about yourself with every new stretch. Try it. It's addictive.

Be Physical

I DON'T THINK I could be the slightest bit productive without an endorphin fix. In fact, this morning before sitting down to work, I ran for about forty-five minutes at sunrise (my favorite time to run). I felt energized and focused when I got back, showered, grabbed some breakfast, and sat down to write. Unless you're addicted to exercise like I am, you may not be able to understand this, but it works for me. I enjoy being physical and I know it's good for me to continue to be active as I age.

I also try to go to the gym at least twice a week. I used to be a full-fledged gym rat and worked out with a personal trainer three times a week, but these days I can barely tolerate spending any time there, especially now that I live in California and the weather is sunny and beautiful all the time. I mean, get real. Who wants to get on an elliptical or treadmill in a stuffy gym when you can be out in the fresh air under a blue sky and surrounded by mountains on one side and ocean on the other? Now I drag myself to the gym, do a short routine with machines and free weights, and leave. But here's the point: I do haul my ass to the gym because I know that strength training is good for me, being physical is good for me. I force myself to go.

This past year, I started dancing with a local group here in Santa Barbara. Although I love to dance and took lessons from the time I was four, I never dreamed that at my age I would be taking classes again.

It's got to be at least thirty years since I've been in a dance class. Not until I saw these women perform to a Queen medley at an outdoor festival did the thought even enter my mind that I would have the opportunity to do this again. They appeared to be a diverse group of women, of different backgrounds and ages, so I thought, *What the heck, I'll approach them once they finish their performance and see what they're all about.* Turns out that anyone who wants to dance can join. I signed up for the next class and started dancing three to four days a week. Because I love to dance, I don't even consider this exercise, but it is and it's a perfect way for me to be physical.

I've gotten to know some of the amazing women in this class. One woman who dances behind me (because we always seem to gravitate to our special spots in class) is eighty-nine! Not only does she consistently show up, but she learns the choreography as well as any of us, maybe better than some. She's fit and always smiling. I never hear her complain about her age or any of the limitations of being almost ninety. She's my inspiration. She knows the power of staying active for a better quality of life. Another source of inspiration for me in this arena is Ruth Bader Ginsburg, who recognized the importance of staying active and worked out with her trainer to maintain her strength and stamina well into her eighties.

Although many of us dutifully go the gym each day out of vanity and fear of losing our muscle tone, another benefit of exercise is that it stimulates brain activity and helps improve cognitive function. Exercise increases your heart rate, which promotes the flow of blood and oxygen to the brain. It also stimulates the production of hormones, which then stimulate the growth of brain cells and cause the hippocampus—the part of the brain vital for memory and learning—to grow in size. This increases our mental function as we age.

The best thing you can do to slow cognitive decline is to be active. And exercise lowers blood pressure and cholesterol, decreases body fat, and builds strong bones and muscles. It reduces physical and emotional stress, anxiety, and depression. Another huge benefit is that physical activity boosts your self-esteem. When you exercise, your body releases endorphins. These chemicals trigger a positive feeling in the body.

If you're invested in staying marketable and keeping your job, one of the best things you can do is get off your ass and be active. It will improve your overall appearance, fitness, and stamina, all of which are important at work. If you look tired and worn out every day, no one will think you're up for the job. You'll be an easy target to push out the door. Exercise helps you perform better, think more clearly, be more optimistic (which we know can be challenging some days). Remember you're fighting the stereotype that "old" means you have little to contribute, that you're stuck in your ways and beyond your expiration date. When you're energized, have a more youthful demeanor, and demonstrate positivity, you'll be less likely to fall into the over-the-hill trap.

So, while you may be motivated to exercise simply to look young and fit (anything that motivates you to be physical is a good thing), a badass woman knows that the best way to stand tall physically, mentally, and emotionally is to keep moving. It also improves your sex life, by the way. Don't discount that benefit.

There are so many options now for workout classes, either in person or online. Today, I saw on YouTube a specific class for "ageless" women to tone up their arms. You can find something for your level that appeals to you, and many online workouts are free. Classes in the gym can lead to friendships. I met some fabulous women in my yoga class. All women around my age, we congregated in the back of the class each week and got to know each other. Soon we'd meet for coffee or breakfast after class.

Plan to be physical. Keep moving and keep moving forward with a positive attitude:

Choose an activity or activities. Do things you enjoy so you'll stick with them. Do you enjoy tennis, golf? Would you enjoy a women's softball league? How about yoga? Hiking? Kayaking? Zumba? Choose an activity and then commit to how many days per week you're willing to do it.

Do it with a buddy. If you're struggling to stay motivated, find an exercise buddy to work out with at the gym or walk, hike, or run with. You're much more likely to stick with a routine when you have a companion and can hold each other accountable.

Find something that works for you. Not interested in the gym or classes? Make a goal to take 10,000 steps a day, lose weight or get into an outfit you've always loved but hasn't fit for a while. Whatever works for you.

Remember Olivia Newton John's "Let's Get Physical"? Do it. Keep moving for your health, your brain, your self-esteem, your appearance, your well-being, your sex life . . . and your career!

Be Present

AT THE RISK of being melodramatic here, I'm going to state, in no uncertain terms, that being present saved my life. I've heard people laud the benefits of being present and sometimes it can sound a little woo-woo, if you know what I mean. And perhaps my story will also strike you as a little "out there," but to me it's very real.

In 2002, my life was pretty normal. I had my daily routine of exercise, work, play, and parenting. Life was good. That being said, I couldn't help but notice that people, lots of people, all strangers, starting coming up to me out of the blue at an alarming rate to warn me that I had a rather large bright-red mark on the back of my right upper arm, a place I couldn't easily see. "Do you know about the mark on the back of your arm?" "Has anyone ever told you that you've got this thing on your arm that doesn't look right?" they would ask. I want to emphasize here that I didn't know these people, had never laid eyes on them before. But they approached me at the gym, in line at the bank, at the grocery store. They literally came out of the woodwork with such concern that I began to worry myself, even though I had been told repeatedly that the thing on my arm was a benign birthmark, nothing to worry about. I could have dismissed their comments, but I didn't. I stayed present and paid attention.

I paid enough attention to schedule an appointment with my internist for a body scan. He looked me over and declared with some confidence that I had nothing to worry about, validating that I had a benign birthmark on my right arm. I could have subsequently dismissed the whole notion that I should be worried, but I didn't. There was something powerful, almost overwhelming, about the number of people who went out of their way to warn me. So, when my internist said to me, "If you want to pursue this, I can refer you to a dermatologist at Yale," I went.

Long story short: two weeks after that appointment with the dermatologist and a biopsy, I got the results. I had malignant invasive melanoma. But here's the kicker. It wasn't on my arm. She found a mole that had irregular borders and varied coloration on my lower right leg.

The message here is hard to miss. I was present. I noticed all the people, complete strangers, who cautioned me that something wasn't right. If I didn't follow up, not once but twice, I probably wouldn't be here to write this today.

Now, I'm not suggesting that a life-changing experience like this will happen to you, and you need to immediately run to the doctor. But what I am advising is to be present in your own life, and at this stage of your career, be present every day you go to work. Show up. Really be there.

It's pretty obvious when someone has checked out at work. I'm sure you're familiar with these people. They go through the motions of showing up, crossing off items on their to-do list for the day, and going home. During the day, they rarely socialize with coworkers or stay engaged at any level. They're permanently "out to lunch." They're not necessarily on the older side, mind you, but they're MIA. They appear bored or disinterested in everything they do. I'm not talking about shy or introverted people here. I'm referring to those employees who have no motivation, those who go through the motions with little interest or energy. Sister, if this is you, you're in trouble. Now isn't the time to pull a Norma Desmond, the aging actress in *Sunset Boulevard*, and retreat to the shadows hoping no one notices you. You can't afford for people to think you're "out to lunch" in any manner of speaking. You need to show you're in the game every day. If it takes a handful of vitamins each morning and going to bed by nine, so be it.

Being present means paying attention to what's going on around you, looking for opportunities to be visible to key stakeholders, sharing your knowledge and ideas with others. It's about raising your hand and offering to help others be successful, making the effort to create meaningful connections with your colleagues, and everything else I talk about in this book. When you're present, you see more potential ways to contribute and prove your value. You also become more keenly aware of the dynamics and behaviors of others, which may help you position yourself going forward. Being present and aware allows you to gather valuable information about the politics, the culture, and which relationships to prioritize.

While you may be pretty upset some days when your workload is redistributed or you hear some rude comments about older workers, resist the pull to check out. Avoid the voice of your inner child saying, *If you're not interested in me, then I'm not going to be interested in you.* Rise above it and show up as your badass self. When you're present, people want to engage with you. They want to collaborate with you and are thrilled to be on your team. Your energy and passion can be inspiring to your colleagues. Remember this. If you check out, you'll get pushed out.

Choose Joy

FEW YEARS AGO, I made a decision to focus on finding joy in my life. I believed I could do much more with my life if I changed my outlook. I was a bit of a worrywart. Not that I normally fretted the day away, but I tended to worry about stuff and that drained my energy. I adopted this frame of mind from my parents, who made worrying an obsession at times. As a child, I often got caught up in their anxiety. But now as an adult with some perspective, I understand that we didn't actually have major issues of a crisis magnitude to cause that much anxiety. Sure, like most middle-class families, my parents worried about money. They worried about their health, which I know is a concern for all of us. But it seemed to me that the negative effects of worrying outweighed what bothered them. That's not a good place to be and that's not how I want to live my life. Yet it's just so easy to fall into that pattern of thinking, especially when that's the dominant mindset of your family. I had to consciously push the worrying out of my life and choose joy.

What really triggered my decision to choose joy, however, was a long bout with Lyme disease in 2016. It was a horrendous year. I felt isolated. I couldn't work, had no energy to exercise or get together with friends. Some days I wandered aimlessly around the house and some days I never made it off the couch. I was losing my identity to this illness every day. I didn't recognize the person I was becoming; I wasn't the gal who got up every morning at five thirty to get to spin class and who enthusiastically coached clients and presented to audiences across the country. I was in a lot of pain, physically and emotionally. And, justifiably so, I was feeling sorry for myself. It was a dark place. Yet it was from this dark place that I chose to escape the doldrums and to live joyfully regardless of circumstances, which, let's face it, you can't always control anyway. I didn't have control of the disease, but I knew I could control my attitude. I decided that I'd rather live the rest of my life in joy than fall into the "oh, woe is me" depression of old age. Wouldn't you? In the end, it was my new joyous attitude that helped me heal from Lyme.

Surprisingly, with this new mindset I discovered that when I switched my filter to seek joy in the world, everything changed. Not that shit doesn't still happen. It does. But choosing joy gave me an entirely different perspective on what's really important. When you look for joy every day, you're no longer dwelling on all the crap in your life. Because, let's face it, we all have our share of negative stuff that we could dwell on if we decided to. Trust me, it could be a full-time job. However, I guarantee that if you look for joy, you'll find it. It's there under the covers perhaps, but it's there. And as if by magic, doors open up for you that you never noticed before. Opportunities for new relationships or new jobs become evident to you, and you gain a great sense of well-being and confidence. With joy comes gratitude and optimism, along with the empowering feeling that you can conquer the world. And if you don't conquer the world, so what? You still have joy in your life.

Think of the joy you feel when you accomplish things you thought were almost impossible, when you overcome obstacles to emerge victorious. Maybe you lost out on a promotion but got another great job in a different department. Perhaps you closed a deal where the cards were stacked against you and everyone thought it would never happen. Acknowledge the joy you feel. Every day you manage to get through some tough shit. Pay attention to your exhilaration. There's joy everywhere if you seek it out.

I find joy each morning when I go for my run at sunrise. I'm acutely aware of the vibrant colors emerging with the sun's first light, the cool air, the joy of being alive in this beautiful place. I celebrate walks on the beach listening to the soothing sound of gentle waves hitting the shore. I rejoice in each visit with my children and grandchildren, and their hugs are beyond description. Pure joy!

This feeling, this joy, promotes your longevity. As you experience joy, your brain releases two chemicals associated with happiness, serotonin and dopamine, into your central nervous system. What happens next is magical. Your circulatory system and your autonomic nervous system are activated. You may flush, your heart may beat a little faster. If you think you feel joy in every cell of your body, you can. Experiencing joy is one of the best prescriptions for you as you age.

As I mentioned before, dancing brings me joy. My parents enrolled me in classes when I was four years old. I remember my first performance, dancing to "I'm a Little Teapot." From that auspicious beginning, I danced all through elementary and middle school, when I still had dreams of becoming a professional ballerina, until I was told that although I was talented, I was too short and not built like a ballerina. In high school, I was dedicated to being on the cheerleading squad and dance took a back seat, but then I picked it up again in college and post-college for a brief period of time. It wasn't until after my second child was born that I found aerobic dancing a great outlet and eventually became an instructor. I wore little white spandex shorts with a T-shirt and leg warmers. Ah, those were the days. I taught about six high-impact aerobics classes a week. I was truly in my joyous place.

But here's what I love about dancing now, at this age. I'm a part of a strong community of women who enjoy dance and bond with each other through music and movement. It's the whole package of dance, music, comradery, and a connection to the wider world through our dances.

In addition to what I've already mentioned, here's the rest of my list of things that bring me joy, in no special order:

- Seeing my children be successful

- Working with my clients

- Listening to music/going to live concerts

- Hanging out with my girlfriends

- Traveling for pleasure to new places/traveling to old familiar places for nostalgia

- Writing without interruption

- Cooking and baking to music

What brings you joy?

Write a list in your journal and create an intention to find joy each day and week. Although some days can seem dismal, joy is there. It may take a little practice on your part to find it at first, but trust me, choosing joy will improve your overall well-being and change your life for the better.

Start
a Journal

HERE'S MY FAVORITE thing about journaling. You can write whatever the hell you want and no one will ever see it, especially if you hide it well from your nosey family. You can rant and rage. You can cuss to your heart's delight in the privacy of your journal pages. If you need a place to express your frustration, anger, and self-pity about your crappy situation at work that no one really wants to hear about, journal. Write it. Feel it, then let it go. It's like a cleanse. Especially when paired with meditation in the morning, it releases all the BS you're carrying with you, without judgment.

But a word to the wise: do not reread and ruminate on your negative entries. That will only fuel your ongoing obsession with whatever triggered your vent in the first place. The only time I reread my past histrionics is after about six months have passed since whatever situation or circumstance upset me at the time. Then I can either celebrate my ability to move on, which makes me feel good about myself, or address the need to write and release a little more, recognizing that I still have work to do because I haven't let go yet.

Journaling reduces stress and anxiety

One of the benefits of journaling, for sure, is to release the toxic bullshit you're carrying with you. And if some of this BS is about work, you need to purge yourself of your heightened emotions in a safe place in order to maintain your sanity and regain your composure, so you can figure out how best to deal with whatever's coming down.

Let's say you have a beef with someone at work. They refer to you as "grandma," call you out as having a stupid idea, or dismiss your opinion as foolish. You're angry, perhaps embarrassed. Are you tempted to let your inner child out of the closet and confront them to their face? Or even get physical because you're so frustrated and mad? Well, that's not going to do you any good and I'm not suggesting you *should* react that way, despite your instinct to tell them off. But what do you do with all that rage? If you hold on to it, it will definitely raise your blood pressure, literally and figuratively. That anger, if not released a bit, may cause you to confront them in a way that doesn't serve you. Sure, you can do something positive, like running a few miles to let it go. You can also do something unhealthy, like binge eating. But you can also write about it. Journaling is a non-impact activity. And by releasing your negative emotions, you're better equipped to deal with upsetting experiences at work that have the potential to derail you if not handled well. It helps you get back on track when the intense feelings have subsided.

Journal for clear thinking

On a positive note, often when I'm rambling in my journal, I discover a new approach to an issue, or in my musings, I'm able to shift my mindset or point of view. I brainstorm with myself in a way and it's a worthwhile exercise. If I try to do all this in my head without writing it out, I get lost in my own thoughts.

Journaling gives you the judgment-free space to think through your ideas. You have to be careful, however, of any effort on your part to sabotage something and toss it out because of your menacing limiting beliefs. For example, say you're considering pitching a new idea at work. You start journaling about it. You get excited and your passion starts to build for this idea, but then as you write, you notice that you're starting to pooh-pooh the idea. *Well, that will never fly because my boss won't listen long enough to hear me out,* or some such negative thought. Now you've lost the clear thinking as you sink into an abyss of self-deprecation and pity. You close your journal and give up on the idea.

If this happens, you have to keep writing until you see a light at the end of the tunnel. Be aware of how you're muddying your clear thoughts with your bullshit. Journal until you're back on track again. That's the beauty of journaling.

Journal to celebrate you and your accomplishments

I love the idea of a success journal, as I recommended in the chapter "Advocate for Yourself and Others." Your journal can be a positive affirmation of wonderful, joyous things that are happening in your life. You managed to slip out of work early enough to catch your daughter's soccer game. You finally dropped the five pounds that you've tried for months to lose. You're feeling really good about recent interactions with your significant other. Celebrate by not only noting the occasion, but also expressing how achieving these things makes you feel. Acknowledge your pride. Brag about yourself to yourself. No one's listening. Let it rip! It's good practice to own your accomplishments.

And if you want to shift to a more positive outlook and build your confidence, journaling your successes will help you convert your default thinking from Debbie Downer to Badass Brianna.

Journal to dream big

Sometimes you just need a safe place to visualize the outrageous dreams that you're embarrassed to share with others or that aren't fully baked and still need time cooking in your head. As you journal about a vision for the future, you're building the courage to take a leap and work toward achieving that goal someday. Or maybe simply describing the dream fuels your creativity. In your journal, you can let your thoughts wander and fill the pages with energy and passion. Your musings don't need to lead to anything more than positive feelings about opportunities yet to be realized in your life. It's joyous and full of promise.

Journal to express gratitude

It's pretty easy to take things for granted. We're busy living our lives after all. I assume that everyone takes things for granted to some degree, at least until a situation presents itself that threatens something or someone we hold dear in our lives: our health, our family, our job, our friendships. Then we're suddenly thrust out of our complacency to understand what life might be like without something or someone we cherish. Journaling to express gratitude encourages your appreciation of everyday occurrences and people in your life. It supports you in being present to embrace all the wonderful things that you normally don't acknowledge.

What a marvelous way to start or finish your day, by expressing gratitude. Honestly, when I do this first thing in the morning, it empowers me and bolsters my energy to live my life fully. When I journal at night, expressing my gratitude helps me sleep better. I fall asleep with a smile on my face.

Whatever you choose to write about, don't worry about spelling and grammar. Just let your thoughts and feelings flow. I prefer handwriting my journal, but there are also online tools if that's your thing. Penzu has a free mobile app option and gives you the opportunity to insert pictures and add tags. Grid Diary gives you a template and questions to answer to inspire your writing if you find it challenging to get started. Day One Journal is free and easy to use as well, and gives you the option of adding video and photos. You could also use Evernote for journaling.

Write and celebrate. Write and release. Write to think clearly. Write to express yourself without judgment. Let it flow. It's pretty badass.

Meditate

DARESAY FEW WOULD proclaim meditating is a badass thing to do. When we think of meditating, we often think of the Dalai Lama, sitting cross-legged for hours, feeling chill. We think of a badass as the antithesis: bold and powerful, fueled with Red Bull energy and intention and challenged to sit still for five minutes. It turns out, however, that meditating is a very badass thing to do. It clears your head, grounds you, settles your emotions, and prepares you to accept what life throws at you. It provides a balance between the calmness necessary to deal with the uncertainty you face at work and the strong connection with your authentic self and your talent that empowers you to take action. Meditation helps you to set your priorities and find a sense of mental stillness in this crazy-intense world we live in. It supports a badass mindset.

I started a meditation practice when I had Lyme disease and felt hopeless and depressed. The harder I tried to get better, the worse I got. Something had to change. I was on a downward spiral. Jennifer, my health care practitioner, suggested meditation and it changed my world. I must confess I'm not very good at it. Because I'm always on the go, usually from early in the morning (and I mean *early* in the morning as a result of recurring insomnia), I find it takes a gargantuan effort to make time to sit quietly and meditate. My mind is active 24/7, constantly distracting me from coming even close to my desired but unrealistic state of enlightenment.

I need to schedule my meditation or it will never happen. That's okay, because most days that intention works for me and if I skip meditating in the morning, I'll often find a few minutes later in the day when I need to step away from work to relax. The chatter in my head never seems to silence for long, so some days I use the Headspace app or Tara Brach's online guided meditation. The gentle voice invites me to relax and focus. I diligently follow the breathing exercise and sit still for fifteen minutes. That's all it takes to refresh my mind and reset my thoughts and feelings.

If you're worried you won't be good at it, forget it. This isn't a competition and no one's judging your performance. The purpose of meditation is to unload all the crap that you tell yourself every day. Although you get better with practice, there's no goal to reach perfection here. It's a practice, and some days it'll go better than others. Don't give up.

Science backs up the benefits of meditation. Believe me, it's not woo-woo. According to research, meditation reduces stress and anxiety and promotes emotional health. It improves your sleep, relaxes your body, and lowers your blood pressure. It decreases depression, reduces loneliness, improves your self-image, and bolsters a positive outlook on life. All of this is critical as we age and when we're filled with self-doubt and question our place in society and at work. Meditation also helps your work performance because it lengthens your attention span and reduces age-related memory loss. It increases your self-awareness and promotes a strong understanding of yourself to be your best self.

Are you sold on it yet? By the way, meditation is also super-convenient. You don't need to go anywhere, and it doesn't cost you a penny. All you need is a quiet space and the intention to do it. *Ommm.*

Love
Yourself

DO YOU THINK of yourself as a best friend or your own worst enemy? Maybe a little bit of both? I guess that's pretty natural, but I think it may be more common, for women especially, to tip the scale toward treating ourselves as enemy number one rather than truly loving and appreciating who we are. And that sucks. I mean, life throws us a lot of crap every day. Do we really need to add self-deprecation and self-loathing to our misery? We expend way too much energy bashing ourselves and that doesn't help our confidence one bit. We beat ourselves up over a whole host of things, especially the unmet and unrealistic expectations that we set for ourselves. Let's face it, we think we need to be perfect, and so we feel unworthy of our love when we don't measure up—which is pretty much all the time because no one's perfect!

One of the most obvious places you may put yourself down is at work, especially now that you've crossed the half-century milestone. If you have a tendency toward perfectionism, beware. This is your danger zone. This is a breeding ground for setting unrealistic high expectations (and I emphasize "unrealistic" here) and then beating yourself up for not meeting them. Your personal put-downs zap your energy and confidence. You think you're unlovable. So, here's where you must shift your perspective. Imagine a world in which you love, honor, and respect yourself. How much more will you enjoy your work and colleagues in this world of love without self-deprecation? Your love and appreciation for who you are fuels your career success.

I know all about the quest to be perfect. Whether or not it was the direct intention of my parents to instill this message growing up, it came across loud and clear. After all, like you, I was rewarded for getting As, looking pretty, being tidy and polite in my younger years. It wasn't until I left for college that I could rebel against this even a little bit. Although it's so ingrained in me, I must admit, it still ain't easy. I struggle to give myself a break. Trudy, my mean inner critic, can annihilate any of the feelings of self-love I nurture in a heartbeat.

Let me tell you, girlfriend, loving yourself is badass, about as badass as you can get. And you need to put your foot down and demand it of yourself. You deserve your love, so stop knocking yourself down and kicking yourself in the gut. Instead, give yourself a kick in the ass and stand up confident and tall. If this doesn't come easily for you, consciously decide to fall in love with yourself.

How do you fall in love with yourself?

Start by listing everything you love about yourself. Forget humility. No one's looking over your shoulder and judging you here. Dig deep. See yourself as others see you. If you need help, ask some close friends to chime in. To get you started, here's my own list of why I'm lovable.

I'm lovable because I'm:

* joyful and optimistic
* smart
* a loyal friend
* playful
* intuitive
* passionate

- persistent yet resilient
- reliable and trustworthy
- creative
- funny
- big- and open-hearted

Just writing this list now makes me feel really good about myself. No bullshit, I'm lovable.

Now open your journal and write down your list. *I'm lovable because...*

Keep your list visible or in your top desk drawer so you can pull it out when you're feeling the urge to put yourself down. The list is a great reminder that you deserve love and respect.

Next, ask yourself what you do for the people you love:

- How do you talk to them?

- Do you pass judgment about their actions or beliefs?

- Are you patient and understanding?

- Are you a good listener?

- Do you regularly hug them?

- Do you compliment them and cheer them up when they're feeling defeated or sad?

- Do you do special things for them to show how much you care?

How many of these things do you do for yourself? Aha! There's the lesson. You need to treat yourself like you would treat your best friend, someone you love. You need to show the same compassion, empathy, patience, and affection. Give yourself a hug right now. You deserve it. You're lovable. xoxo

Put Yourself First

I F YOU'RE LIKE most women I know, you spend a boatload of time trying to please everyone. Not only is this an exercise in frustration, but also it is a surefire way to sabotage your career success. First of all, not everyone is going to like you no matter how hard you try. So, forget about that. Please yourself first and if people don't sing your praises, that's their problem. Letting go of the desire to be universally liked is a lesson in badassery.

The bottom line here is that putting others first and yourself last needs to end right now. It's your time and you have to claim it. You've spent decades with your head down working hard or running around like a chicken with its head cut off trying to balance your work with your family, social, and volunteer commitments. And in doing so, inevitably, you've come last, every time.

For me, one of the blessings about getting older is that my children are grown and out of the house, busy with their own lives. I now have the time and space to prioritize *me* and do things for myself I never dared to dream about when I was younger. When I was a single mom trying to navigate my career, grabbing time for myself was hard because there literally was no time, and if there was, I felt guilty even thinking about putting myself first, let alone acting on it.

We're programmed from childhood to be self-sacrificing women. The smallest notion of straying from this lifestyle comes with tons of guilt, whether you are a mother or not. Know any guys like that? If I were a betting woman, I'd say not likely. I am not suggesting that you have to become an overnight narcissist, but come on, surely there's a middle ground where you can do better about prioritizing yourself, at least some of the time.

If you're ambitious and trying to move up in the workplace, you might be compelled by the desire to get everyone to like you by compromising who you are. As you grow older and find yourself compromised by others, you feel desperate to please everyone to keep your job. As a result, you're overly cautious. You hold yourself back. You hesitate to offer ideas and opinions for fear others will disagree with you. You don't advocate for yourself because people will think you're full of yourself. You get the idea, right? Everyone else becomes a priority. What they may think overrides your opinions. What they may need supersedes what you need. This is a recipe for career disaster.

What would you do for yourself if you made yourself a priority? Do you know? Have you ever given yourself the luxury of self-reflective time to figure this out?

I'm not suggesting you quit your job and take off for Bali. (Although some days that seems like an excellent idea!) I'm suggesting that you think about who you are and what you really want and need at this point in your life. Are you compromising yourself to remain in your current job? What price are you paying for doing so? Do you have panic attacks, anxiety, or high blood pressure as a result of work? Do you want to wait it out until you can retire or they fire you?

If you choose to stay in your current job, you're deciding that because your job and/or salary are of primary importance. And even though you may feel disrespected and marginalized, you're willing to stick it out. Again, no judgment. However, you needn't give all your power away in doing so. Recognize that you have decided consciously and, as long as the choice is not fear-based, you will be okay with the status quo. Wear your Teflon armor to work and don't lower yourself by getting caught up in the negativity of the workplace. Remind yourself that you are *choosing* to stay given the circumstances. You're taking full advantage of the salary and benefits for the time being. Stand by your decision until it makes sense to leave.

Rita, one of my former clients, examined her priorities and concluded that for her it makes sense to stick it out at the tech company where's she been employed for fifteen years. Despite the humiliation and frustration of being marginalized, she realizes how difficult it will be to find another position as a fifty-eight-year-old woman attorney. She continues to network with former colleagues, although her heart isn't in looking for work right now. She earns a great salary, has a generous benefits package, and will remain on the job as long as they keep her. However, she also focuses on activities outside work to help her to feel good about herself. She loves hiking, her daily visit to the gym, and meetups with girlfriends. Doing what makes her feel good balances the bad vibes from work. Right now, it works for her. Her decision. She's staying but on her terms.

When I didn't receive the promotion I wanted and was offered a lateral position instead, it would have been easy to stay put. After all, I was forty-nine years old and had been with the company eight years and knew the ropes. But I also knew that I had more value than the organization recognized. (Or they would have given me the promotion, right?) I believed in myself and felt it was worth the gamble to leave, move to Chicago, and run a company where I basically had to start over. It was risky but, first and foremost, I believed in myself.

How do you move yourself to the top of the list? This question might be unsettling if you've never, ever made yourself number one. Or maybe you tried but found yourself drowning in guilt, so you decided it wasn't worth it. Or maybe you were overcome with fear that people wouldn't like you. And if people don't like you, then how will you be successful at work.

Old habits are damn hard to break, and if you've never put yourself first, even the idea of doing this can cause heart palpitations. If you're fifty-, sixty-, seventy-plus... geez, that's decades of self-sacrifice and taking a back seat. So, let's start simple. I tell my clients all the time to "chunk it down" and take baby steps when something's overwhelming. Take some baby steps with me.

Ask yourself this: How would you advise your best friend to put herself first? Talk to yourself like you are your own BFF. In your journal, write yourself a letter of permission that looks something like this:

Dear Bonnie,

I want to acknowledge how special you are and what an amazing mother, grandmother, and friend you are. (OMG, this isn't easy to write.) As your BFF, I can always count on your encouragement and support. I've witnessed how you go out of your way for others.

But it's about time you put yourself first. You've always worked hard, but, girlfriend, you need to recognize that life is pretty damn short and you're already past midway. Do you want to take a back seat the rest of your life?

What's on your bucket list? Let's plan something special to do together. Because we deserve it! You deserve it.

Your best friend forever,

ME XOXOXO

Whew! That wasn't easy, but now I feel pretty good. My BFF (me) is right. I do deserve to put myself first—not necessarily all the time, but even occasionally will be a huge improvement. I get that it takes practice to do this, and I'm ready to venture into this strange territory. I've already spent most of my life somewhere near the end of my priority list, and that's enough.

Seek support from your loved ones, who I'm sure will agree that this is important for your confidence and well-being. Maybe as a first step, you find a girlfriend willing to go on a special adventure with you—a spa day, a goddess retreat, a weekend getaway—or who will be there for you as you take this brave leap into the front seat. Share your feelings of insecurity and guilt with her and also in your journal. If this is new behavior for you, guilt will certainly rear its ugly head. Be prepared and armor yourself with your permission letter and encouragement from close friends. Putting yourself first is long overdue. You paid your dues, now reap the rewards. You are number one!

Choose the Glass Half Full

I KNOW A FEW Debbie Downers, although I try to avoid them as much as possible because they drain my energy. You can almost see the dark cloud over their heads. They frustrate the hell out of me, and I tolerate their fatalistic negativity only in small doses. Very small doses. Where I see opportunities, they see problems. When I'm excited, they feel compelled to warn me of potential doom and gloom. I mean, who needs this in their life?

Let me tell you: attitude is everything, especially with aging. The way I look at it is that I have a limited time on Earth and only one life, so why waste my energy looking at everything through a dark lens? I'm not suggesting that we look at life only through rose-colored glasses, though. We need to be balanced and have at least one foot on the ground.

When it comes to growing old, do I need a Debbie Downer pointing out all the bad things that result from aging? I acknowledge things are changing. I realize my tummy is more flabby than flat, that I need help reading the small print. I have crow's feet and a bit of a double chin. I know I don't have the energy I once had. It's reality. But here's what's important: I can control whether or not it controls me. We create our own reality and that reality can be positive or negative.

So, the questions become: How do I want to live the rest of my years on this planet? Do I wallow in self-pity because I'm getting old or am I grateful that I'm getting old? Am I so worried about my future that I forget to live in the present?

If you have a positive mindset about life, it works in your favor. For one thing, a lot of evidence suggests that a positive attitude improves your health and helps you recover faster from serious illness or surgery. An optimistic mindset gives you the feeling that you have some control over your life. When you're hopeful, you not only feel good but you have the energy and determination to live with passion. Again, the glass-half-full mindset isn't a clueless, "everything is wonderful" la-la land attitude. It's a realistic desire to tackle life's problems as adventures, as opportunities, where perhaps you'll stumble at times, but in the end you'll be okay. You trust that despite some hurdles, you'll survive, maybe even thrive. The trust in positivity is the key.

Now you may think, *Bonnie, whenever I hope that something will turn out okay, I set myself up for disappointment*. Well, sure. Not everything's easy. Not everything has a happy ending. I get that. It's not advisable to be a Naive Nora and lose all touch with reality. But if you adopt the glass-half-full mindset and things do not go as you wish, you pick yourself up faster and get on with your life. You're not preoccupied with waiting for the other shoe to drop. You see the experience as a life lesson and remain optimistic that there are still great things for you around the corner. And when you think this way, you spot the many options that are out there for you.

A positive mindset at work functions much the same way. Maybe you didn't get the promotion or raise you wanted, yet you still believe there are opportunities for you to contribute value and get recognition. That attitude increases your awareness to see and seize opportunities. It improves your productivity and decision-making. With a glass half full, you show up at work with the energy to take on your projects and face any challenges. Your manager and colleagues feel your positivity, want to work with you, and are eager to support your efforts. You are keen to learn new things and optimistic about your future, excited to continue to invest in your career. A positive mindset also helps you deal with conflict and negative feedback. You become more resilient.

If you view circumstances only through a negative lens, you simply cannot see an upside to anything. You fall into the victim trap, which paralyzes you from being productive. You set yourself up to be pushed out because people don't want to be around you.

I see how this plays out every day with my clients and with the many women I've talked to at my workshops and conferences. Some have gone through hard times. They've been humiliated at work because of their age, and they've been shown the door. In some cases, the experience of being fired or demoted is traumatic. But it's interesting to observe who recovers and pulls themselves together to find another job more easily. Women who believe the glass is half full and believe in their value use their positive attitude to network, refine their résumé, and jump into the job market with confidence that gets their careers back on track. One such woman is Pamela.

Pamela moved to New York City for a job in a financial services firm. Burdened with hefty grad-school loan payments, a new job with a salary lower than what she'd earned in San Francisco, and increased expenses, she said to herself, *I can make this work*. But just eight short months later, the firm laid her off. She had very little savings, that student debt, and of course living expenses. She needed a new job, and fast.

Pamela admitted to me she was scared at the time. But she kept saying to herself, *Don't be—you can make this work*. During her job search, while doing temp work, she was invited by a dear friend to apply for a communications role at her company. Up to that point, Pamela had no interest in communications; her background was in institutional trading, commodities futures and options, and asset management. And besides that, she wasn't sure she could do communications. After all, she never had before.

When she was offered the job, she had a "flash of fear," but she took the offer, thinking she'd give it six months and then reassess. Now, years later, she's an officer and head of communications at a bank in New York and loving her career. She knows that no matter what happens, she can always reinvent herself if she wants or needs to. Her mantra is "to say yes to the unknown, and so what if I fail? That just gets me closer to what works. I'm not scared anymore."

Sometimes, it takes awhile after a traumatic firing to rediscover that positivity, but Sally Koslow's story demonstrates that it's worth being patient and dealing with all your emotions before you move on. Sally was at the peak of her career as editor in chief at *McCall's* magazine. But she was totally blindsided when the magazine asked her to step aside because they were launching a new magazine for Rosie O'Donnell. Sally was booted upstairs to take on some meaningless job and then seven months later she was fired.

Though devastated, Sally bounced back: "I followed every Rx for landing a job—cheerfully networked, even wrote a magazine article about resiliency and followed my own advice. Within months I got rehired into what for me was a dream job: inventing a magazine." Sally wholeheartedly embraced this new position, working long hours. She loved every minute, but after almost three years she was called into the office of the head of HR with her boss and told they were going in a different direction. She'd just turned fifty.

Sally was "stunned, pulverized." This time she didn't bounce right back. She was depressed and doubted herself: "Would employers start to think I was untalented, or judge me harshly in an industry where a long résumé is code for stale and the old boys club had morphed into the young girls club?"

After some time passed, tired of lunches and coffees with girlfriends, Sally realized she needed some structure to her day. She took control of her life and enrolled in a writing workshop. From that workshop, a new career was born for Sally, that of a novelist. Sally has written six successful novels to date. Pretty badass, I'd say.

Sally's story illustrates that when life deals you a couple of bad hands, it sucks. It's real. It's not always easy to be positive. I get it. It can be challenging to find yourself and rediscover your passion and energy after you've been knocked down repeatedly. But here's the thing: with patience and positivity, new doors open.

If you're more of an Eeyore and find all this glass-half-full stuff challenging, here's another exercise to get over your negative outlook. List three to five things you're negative about and reframe them with a positive plan and perspective. For example:

- My relationship with my manager isn't great, but I'm actively working on how to improve it.

- I'm worried that I'll lose my job, but I have a strategic plan in case I'm terminated before retirement.

- I've been out of touch with people in my network for too long to reach out, but I'm actively reconnecting and building my network now to ensure that I have opportunities if I'm let go.

A positive outlook creates forward momentum, and that is badass. Remember there's a bright side despite how dismal things may seem. Perhaps you'll find work at a better company. Maybe you'll start a business of your own or begin a whole new career. A glass-half-full attitude will open doors that a negative one will close. Are you with me on this?

Hang with
Your Girlfriends

HONESTLY DON'T KNOW what I'd do without my girlfriends. Family is important. Spouses and partners are important. But girlfriends are essential for me to maintain my emotional equilibrium and sanity, especially as I age. With my girlfriends, I feel comfortable sharing my most intimate thoughts without fear of judgment. We can laugh together about our experiences with aging. My friends grant me a safe zone in which I can let my hair down and cry. Day by day, we laugh, sometimes uncontrollably, and find joy in being together. Girlfriends are the best!

As I've mentioned before, I don't have a huge group of friends. I prefer an intimate circle. And each of my friends offers me a different perspective on life. I treasure their sound advice, which comes with no agenda other than my well-being. They listen. They have patience. They're loving and supportive. And I respond in kind.

That give-and-take in friendship strengthens the bond. As my colleague Kare Anderson, author and TED Talk speaker, rightly notes, mutuality matters. It matters whether you're developing alliances in or out of work. When you listen to others and make a gesture to help or add value, the bond is created. And it is gratifying. This is the kind of stuff that makes us feel needed and appreciated on a deep level.

And as women, we know this. To help others and be there for others is in our DNA.

With all this said, it's no surprise then that hanging with your girlfriends is good for your mental and physical health. Although you probably don't need proof because you feel it yourself, studies demonstrate the benefits of friendship in these areas. Plus the research confirms that socializing improves your happiness and positivity. It helps you deal with stress and calms you down. Some recommend that you hang with your girlfriends twice a week. I wish I could do this regularly but life sometimes gets in the way, and I'm not geographically close to all my dearest friends. However, weekly and sometimes daily check-in calls are important to me. FaceTime makes it even more personal. I've even arranged for my college friends to have a virtual happy hour over Zoom. It works great to keep us connected.

When things get dicey at work, an objective ear from someone outside your workplace is a blessing. Many of my friends are entrepreneurs and we share our work challenges. If you have a trusted girlfriend at work, you can use each other as sounding boards to get through the tough times. Schedule times to get together during work or after hours.

Spending time with friends seems to be an innate behavior for women and one that extends our life expectancy. According to research out of UCLA, "women more reliably turn to their social contacts in times of stress, responses that are ... protective of health and longevity. The fact that men may be somewhat more likely to cope with stress via fight or flight and women to cope with stress via tend and befriend may help to explain the worldwide gender gap in mortality." Wow! There you have it. Hanging with your girlfriends helps you live longer.

Socializing with friends helps older women deal with loneliness and depression, according to a report in *Psychology Today* that states that "female friendships can be the key to happiness in older women, but they're not often treated as such." And it's true: we hear a lot more about the importance of exercise and nutrition than hanging out with girlfriends.

In need of finding some like-minded women? You may want to consider some groups that focus on women over forty-five, like NextTribe: The Voice of Women Aging Boldly, to share the experiences and challenges of aging with articles, virtual and live events, as well as fun trips; or the CoveyClub, which supports women's advancement and growth after forty. There are many Facebook groups around special interests such as writing and book clubs. And consider joining some local meetups to run, walk, hike, or socialize for wine tastings, art walks, and so on. Believe me, women out there are also eager to connect.

When Dale Pollekoff moved to Los Angeles in her seventies and wanted to make new friends, she found it difficult. Meeting people in LA isn't easy. Frustrated that all the Meetup groups were for young women, Dale started her own, Finding Female Friends Past Fifty. As of this writing, the group has more than 2,700 members. It turns out that many women out there are looking for female friends. If you can't find a group, organize one!

Bottom line: if you don't regularly socialize with your friends, you need to consciously plan to spend time with them or seek new friends. Especially as you get older and may live alone, your friendships are your connection to the world, often your connection to reality. I'm so grateful to have so many special women in my life—old friends going back to elementary school and new friends I've met on the West Coast. My girlfriends are my rock and I treasure them.

Own the
Power of Your Age

WHAT BATTLES HAVE you fought and won? You don't get to be fifty or older without baggage. We all have trunks full of it, and memories, good and bad, of what it's taken for us to get to where we are today. Our life journey is enriched with all the wonderful experiences that have molded us into who we are. And as much as we may focus on our aging and our current status and present circumstances at work, we are the sum total of decades of life and career ups and downs. That's who we are. And we need to acknowledge and celebrate all of it. We need to honor our journey, our successes, our missteps, and how we've managed to overcome all the obstacles life has presented over the years. This is the power of our experience, the power of our age.

I was divorced at thirty-four with two children, six and eight. Because I got married in grad school, post-divorce was the first time I was on my own. And I was responsible for two children as well as myself. My ex took the kids some weekends, but most of the parenting responsibility was mine. I had to buy a house, relocate, and set up a new household. I moved to a town where I knew no one and settled the kids in a new school, where they knew no one. I needed to find another job because my teaching position didn't provide enough income to cover my expenses. I took an entry-level position in a new field that eventually led me to the C-suite. That's pretty badass, right?

Laura, whom I mentioned earlier, was forced out of her managing director position after twenty-two years of solid performance. It was devastating and humiliating to be chastised at work and then terminated. This experience could have sidelined her; it might have stoked her fears that at fifty she was too old to compete. She could have become so fearful of getting another job that she didn't apply for a comparable position, aiming low just to be safe. But that's not what happened. Laura pulled herself together and put herself out there. And guess what? She landed another great job with a company that appreciates her contributions and she's thriving there. That's badass.

Sally Koslow could have taken her pink slip from *McCall's* magazine as a sign that her career was over, but she reinvented herself to become a successful author. That's badass.

I've spoken to many women over fifty who have left their companies or were let go, and who are starting businesses, going back to school, finding ways to remain marketable. This takes chutzpah. It's not easy to change careers at this age. But they're doing it and surviving, and leading fulfilling lives despite disappointments. When these women were let go, they found new work, new careers in some cases, that they probably wouldn't have had they not been forced out. They wear their battle scars well.

My point here is that we never think of any of this as special. We do what it takes to survive in life. At times, I reflect on my own experiences and wonder how the hell I did it. I wasn't a perfect parent. I made mistakes. I did my best. But I did it. And we all do it! We do what we need to do to get by and hopefully thrive. We've all overcome challenges in our lives and emerged stronger for the journey. Celebrating each accomplishment, big and small, is important. Because we don't. We take it for granted that anyone could do what we do.

Acknowledging the challenges you've overcome is where you find your inner badass. She's just waiting to be discovered.

At this stage in your life, it's more important than ever to honor your journey and own the power of your age. Let's create a list of the battles you've fought and won, and include a high five for overcoming the challenge. Here are some of mine:

- I survived a divorce that left me without many financial resources and I built a successful career from scratch. *Kudos to me!*

- I've been single for more than thirty years and I raised my kids, reasonably well, and balanced that with a career. *Whew, that wasn't easy but I did it.*

- I've had several major career disappointments but managed to keep myself on track emotionally and move on with confidence and optimism. *That's taken a lot of grit and resilience.*

- I've survived some devastating illnesses by myself and pulled together all my strength and badass belief in the future to maintain my health. *Sometimes I had to dig deep to stay positive, but I did it.*

Now write your list of battles you've fought and won and your high fives. Try this exercise with a friend or group of friends and celebrate each other's victories.

How does it feel when you read your list?

My guess is you feel pretty good after doing this exercise. Toss aside any self-deprecating thoughts about anyone being able to do what you've done. The fact is that *you* did it. Yes, that's right. You are a warrior. Pretty badass, I'd say. Keep adding to this list and acknowledge your ongoing wins. As you celebrate your ability to overcome the many challenges you've faced, you gain a sense of who you truly are beyond any ageist assumptions that may limit you now. You gain more power to dismiss them and realize that you can do pretty much anything you set your mind to do. Never take your ability to persist or your resilience for granted. Use all this positive energy to boost your confidence and inspire you to fight your present and future battles. Be badass. March on!

Move from Sadass to Badass

WORDS MATTER. WORDS are powerful. Author Yehuda Berg says, "Words are singularly the most powerful force available to humanity. We can choose to use this force constructively with words of encouragement, or destructively using words of despair. Words have energy and power with the ability to help, to heal, to hinder, to hurt, to harm, to humiliate, and to humble." Yet, in truth, we rarely understand the influence our words have on others and especially on ourselves.

Without words, our thoughts can't become reality. Words describe our moods, our opinions, and our emotions. When we say we're pissed, people get it. When we use words to let others know we love them or we're disappointed, they understand what we're feeling, perhaps in a way they could not before hearing the descriptors. Words enable us to communicate with others and build relationships. But most importantly, we use words to describe to ourselves who we are and our future path. Words have the ultimate power of influencing a life of positivity or one of difficulty and despair.

For example, how many times have you described yourself as "forgetful," "unattractive," "over the hill"? We use a whole litany of negative adjectives, unaware that in doing so we diminish ourselves and deflate our egos and confidence. These adjectives rob us of our power and influence. Yet we have a powerful choice to instead use words that empower us and support us to create a successful career and fulfilling life. Yeah, it all starts with our thoughts and word choices.

In my own life, I realized that from time to time the stories I told myself were the biggest obstacles to the career and life I wanted. My stories have changed over time, but during different periods of my life, they chastised me, squashed my optimism, and destroyed my confidence. I had a "woe is me" story after a breakup. That story was full of self-pity and grief and an overwhelming feeling of not being lovable. I lived in that story until I was able to write a new one in which I appreciated and loved myself. Other times, I told myself that I was a mediocre author and no one would want to read my book (the one that you're reading now—thank you very much). That story caused me to put writing on hold and shelve my life purpose. Luckily, that story didn't survive long before I created another, more positive one. I told myself that I was a terrible mother. That was probably the most painful story of all. All of my hurtful stories began during different times in my life and kept me from owning my brilliance and authenticity.

I started to see a pattern emerge, not only with myself but with my clients. Our stories were sabotaging us. It's not enough that we're dealing with sexism and ageism, we pile our own shit on top and destroy any hope of remaining whole. When I recognized that my clients' stories about themselves were holding them back, and that they had no clue they were doing this to themselves, I gave them an exercise. I told them to write down the current story they tell themselves about themselves. More often than not, their narrative was a startling eye-opener. Yikes! They'd see the significance right away. "This story is slowly killing me. How can I possibly have the career and life I want if I'm basically telling myself every day that I'm stupid and fat and irrelevant?" And that's the point. If your story doesn't support your success, how can you be successful?

I gave this assignment to a talented and attractive thirty-eight-year-old client from Switzerland. This was her story:

> *I am just surviving. I have no purpose or motivation in life. I am not taken seriously or respected by anyone—my partner, my colleagues, my family, or friends. I am incapable and superficial. I am a procrastinator. I am fat and old. I'm ill and can't sleep well.*

I was shocked and I think she was as well. Did you catch the part that she thought she was old at thirty-eight? I asked her point-blank, "Does this story serve you?" Obviously, her response was no, not at all. But it was her reality. She lived this story and it prevented her from stepping up in her career and her relationships.

The next step was for her to write a new story, a positive and empowering story about how she felt when she adopted a badass mindset. It went like this:

> *I am thriving. I have purpose and motivation in my life. I make progress every day. I am recognized by my partner, my colleagues, my family, and my friends. I am capable and profound. I get things done and make things happen. I have options. I am fit and young. I am healthy and sleep well.*

I began to witness her transformation. She read her story out loud each day. She kept it visible. Her new story began to fuel her ambition, success, and well-being.

Now it's your turn to write your story. Be brutally honest. That's the only way this exercise really works. In as much detail as possible, write your current story—not what you would like it to be but what you *actually* tell yourself about yourself, every day. Write it as you live it, in first person. Get in touch with your words, your reality, and let it flow.

Read your story. What did you learn? Does your story support or sabotage your present and your future? Take a minute. This can be a pretty emotional exercise. Breathe in. Let it out. This is what you see as your truth right now. More than likely, the story you tell yourself about yourself undermines your success.

Breathe in and let it out. Breathe and let go of this shit. Now is the time to write a new, empowering story to propel you forward. If your current story is sadass, make it badass. You control this.

Write your new story with attention to detail in first person, present tense as if you're already living it. "I *am*." Not "I *will*." You might want to answer some of these questions: What kind of work are you doing? How do you feel doing that work? What are your relationships like with your family, friends, colleagues, significant other? What do you want them to be? How does that feel? Carefully choose your words for the feeling they create and find the adjectives that give you joy and confidence.

My story today is:

I wake up each morning early, make my coffee and have a quick cup before I head out for a run. The air is fresh and cool and the smell of jasmine envelops me. I'm overwhelmed with joy at the beautiful sunrise. I'm excited about my day of coaching clients and writing. I love helping my clients push through their barriers and own their talent. Their successes are the fuel for me to go on and help others.

Midday I stop to express my gratitude and meditate. I feel grounded and purposeful and set my intention for the remainder of the day. My day is productive and creative.

As you write your new story, don't jump to solutions. Don't concern yourself with how things will happen, but stay in the positive space and welcome in the good feelings that accompany the new story. And, most importantly, don't immediately judge the story as a pipe dream. Stay with it. Stay with the positive, powerful emotions until you finish writing it. And then read it out loud every day. This story becomes your new mantra. And as you repeat it daily, you begin to own it and live it. From sadass to badass, it's your new story.

Conclusion:
You've Got This,
Girlfriend

YOU KNOW WHAT? I feel really positive about you and your future. I know you can help yourself be bigger, braver, and bolder to overcome all the challenges you face in life and in the workplace.

For some of you, any change in attitude may be an abrupt about-face because you've realized through our journey together that you were headed in the wrong direction—or, worse, maybe downhill. But you caught yourself in time and have done the work to pull yourself out of your "woe is me" fifty-, sixty-, or seventy-year-old rut. You can see clearly how you were getting caught up in all the ageist bullshit and how it was depleting you of your energy, zest for life, and ambition.

Maybe some of you just needed a little reminder that you have everything you need to thrive. We all need to regularly remind ourselves of how amazing we are. You've learned that you absolutely don't need to wish the years and wrinkles away. You've learned the power of owning, loving, and honoring who you are. You're smart and experienced and have a lot to offer your friends, your family, your company, and the world. It's taken decades to gain this knowledge and now it's your time to find your voice and share this wisdom. Respect who you are and your history as well as your future.

I know you are not anywhere *close* to being done yet. I believe in you. And I know that the world will be better off as you step up and act for yourself and on behalf of other girls and women everywhere.

You've got this, girlfriend.

Acknowledgments

GENDERED AGEISM in the workplace is a topic that I've wanted to write about for a couple of years. Passionate about exposing the bias and how it affects women fifty-plus, I initially struggled to find my voice and the right approach. With the support of Sophfronia Scott, I was able to create a book that is informative yet personal. Sophfronia guided me through this delicate process.

Page Two has been an enthusiastic partner in creating this book. My special thanks to cofounder Trena White, my editor Kendra Ward, and the whole team. It's been a joy working with you.

I'm also grateful to the team at Weaving Influence, especially Christy Kirk and Becky Robinson, for their encouragement to write this book. With their expertise, I started my podcast, *Badass Women of Any Age*, to highlight inspiring stories of women owning their courage and stepping into their workplace power.

I also want to thank the women who came forward to be interviewed for this book. Subjected to ageism, sexism, and sometimes termination, they bravely offered their stories so that other women in this demographic can avoid being blindsided and pushed out.

Notes

I'm Too Old to Compete

"Christie Ciraulo and her team . . . in the open water": Bonnie Marcus,
"Christie Ciraulo and the Mighty Mermaids Never Give Up," *Badass Women
at Any Age* (podcast), December 17, 2019, 34:25, https://badasswomen.
libsyn.com/012-christie-ciraulo-and-the-mighty-mermaids-never-give-up.

I'm No Longer Attractive

"attractiveness positively affects income": Jaclyn S. Wong and Andrew M.
Penner, "Gender and the Returns to Attractiveness," *Social Stratification
and Mobility* 44 (June 2016): 113–23, https://doi.org/10.1016/j.rssm.2016.
04.002.
"The global antiaging market": "Anti-aging Market (Breast Augmentation,
Liposuction, Anti-wrinkle Products and Hair Restoration)—Global
Industry Analysis and Forecast 2020–2025," Market Research Engine,
January 2020, https://www.marketresearchengine.com/reportdetails/
anti-aging-market-report.
"in 2017 alone, over $16 billion was spent": 2017 *Plastic Surgery Statistics
Report*, American Society of Plastic Surgeons, 2017, https://www.plastic
surgery.org/documents/News/Statistics/2017/plastic-surgery-statistics-
full-report-2017.pdf.

"dedicated an entire book to her aging, sagging neck": Nora Ephron, *I Feel Bad About My Neck: And Other Thoughts on Being a Woman* (New York: Alfred A. Knopf, 2006).

I Need to Look Young to Succeed

"Lois Frankel . . . 'but for some people' ": Lois Frankel, interview with the author, June 7, 2018.

"we face age discrimination earlier than men": "Gendered Ageism: Trend Brief," Catalyst, October 17, 2019, https://www.catalyst.org/research/gendered-ageism-trend-brief.

I'm Powerless over My Present and Future

"The most common way": Alice Walker, "The most common way people give up their power . . ." Brainyquote, accessed July 10, 2020, https://www.brainy-quote.com/quotes/alice_walker_385241.

I'll Never Get Another Job

"The struggle for women . . . even lower for middle-aged women": Teresa Ghilarducci, "Why Women Over 50 Can't Find Jobs," PBS New Hour, January 14, 2016, https://www.pbs.org/newshour/economy/women-over-50-face-cant-find-jobs.

"(ADEA) of 1967": "Age Discrimination in Employment Act of 1967," U.S. Equal Employment Opportunity Commission, accessed July 10, 2020, https://www.eeoc.gov/statutes/age-discrimination-employment-act-1967.

I'm Terrified of Aging

"positive self-perceptions about getting older": "Thinking Positively about Aging Extends Life More Than Exercise and Not Smoking," YaleNews, July 29, 2002, https://news.yale.edu/2002/07/29/thinking-positively-about-aging-extends-life-more-exercise-and-not-smoking.

"that mindset affects your health": "How the Aging Brain Affects Thinking," National Institute on Aging, May 17, 2017, https://www.nia.nih.gov/health/how-aging-brain-affects-thinking.

Declare Your Ambition

"older workers are just as motivated and reliable as their younger colleagues":
Nathaniel Reade, "The Surprising Truth About Older Workers," AARP,
updated September 2015, https://www.aarp.org/work/job-hunting/info-07-
2013/older-workers-more-valuable.html.

"a rise in ambition": "New Study by Women's Success Coaching Reveals Key
to Gender Gap in the C-Suite," PR Web, September 21, 2016, http://www.
prweb.com/releases/2016/09/prweb13697440.htm.

Advocate for Yourself and Others

"women in the West Wing of the White House": Juliet Eilperin, "White
House Women Want to Be in the Room Where It Happens," *Washington
Post*, September 16, 2016, https://www.washingtonpost.com/news/
powerpost/wp/2016/09/13/white-house-women-are-now-in-the-room-
where-it-happens.

"a repeated and consistent practice of positive thinking": Nate Klemp, "The
Neuroscience of Breaking Out of Negative Thinking (and How to Do It in
Under 30 Seconds)," Inc.com, accessed July 10, 2020, https://www.inc.com/
nate-klemp/try-this-neuroscience-based-technique-to-shift-your-mindset-
from-negative-to-positive-in-30-seconds.html?cid=search.

Cultivate Your Growth Mindset

"the brain is elastic and supple": Jeffrey Kluger, "You're Never Too Old,"
Time Special Edition, The Science of Creativity (New York: Time Books, Inc.,
2018), 81.

"subjects scored highest in their inductive reasoning": Ravenna Helson and
C. J. Soto, "Up and Down in Middle Age: Monotonic and Nonmonotonic
Changes in Roles, Status, and Personality," *Journal of Personality and
Social Psychology* 89, no. 2 (2005): 194–204. https://doi.org/10.1037/0022-
3514.89.2.194.

Be Politically Savvy

"how women feel about office politics": Bonnie Marcus, *The Politics of Promotion: How High-Achieving Women Get Ahead and Stay Ahead* (New York: Wiley, 2015).

Dress the Part

"Scarlett DeBease... "'less makeup is better as you get older'": Scarlett DeBease, interview with the author, June 20, 2018.

Respond to Ageist Comments without Getting Fired

"Being a mom...aspects of family": Nancy Pelosi quoted in Dana Bash, "Nancy Pelosi: 'I Want Women to See That You Do Not Get Pushed Around," CNN, updated November 13, 2018, https://www.cnn.com/2018/11/13/politics/nancy-pelosi-badass-women-washington/index.html.

Know Your Rights

"when you experience age discrimination... 'that I am experiencing'": Davida Perry, interview with the author, February 16, 2019.

"After the meeting... as Perry suggests": Davida Perry, interview with the author, February 16, 2019.

"You want to... 'what this is really about'": Laurie Berke-Weiss, interview with the author, June 20, 2018.

"Congress enacted the Age Discrimination in Employment Act": "Age Discrimination in Employment Act of 1967," U.S. Equal Employment Opportunity Commission, accessed July 10, 2020, https://www.eeoc.gov/statutes/age-discrimination-employment-act-1967.

""There is no law'... considered illegal": Patricia Barnes, *Overcoming Age Discrimination in Employment: An Essential Guide for Workers, Advocates & Employers* (self-published, 2016), 1, 142–43.

"I do think... talking to an attorney": Margaret Kreeger, interview with the author, July 12, 2018.

"Ask yourself... when you might have retired": Carol Frohlinger, interview with the author, March 10, 2019.

Land a New Job

"Linda Descano... 'resilience, and a can-do attitude'": Linda Descano, inter-
    view with the author, May 26, 2020.

Be Your Badass Self

"stands up for herself...": InStyle (@Instyle), "What makes a badass? 'A badass
    woman stands up for herself, is confident, and is not afraid to challenge
    the hierarchy, the patriarchy, or conventional thinking,'" Twitter, June 26,
    2018, 1:26 p.m., https://twitter.com/InStyle/status/1011662014157074433/
    photo/1.

Get Out of Your Comfort Zone

"Life begins...": Yubing Zhang, "Life Begins at the End of Your Comfort Zone,"
    TEDxStanford, June 18, 2015, video, 9:36, https://youtu.be/cmN4x0GkxGo.

Be Physical

"The best thing you can do to slow cognitive decline": David J. Linden, "The
    Truth Behind 'Runner's High' and Other Mental Benefits of Running,"
    Johns Hopkins Medicine, accessed July 10, 2020, https://www.hopkins
    medicine.org/health/wellness-and-prevention/the-truth-behind-runners-
    high-and-other-mental-benefits-of-running.

Choose Joy

"As you experience joy... beat a little faster": "This Is How Joy Affects Your
    Body," Healthline, accessed July 10, 2020, https://www.healthline.com/
    health/affects-of-joy#3.

Meditate

"meditation reduces stress... outlook on life": Madhuleena Roy Chowdhury,
    "5 Health Benefits of Daily Meditation According to Science," Positive
    Psychology.com, May 18, 2020, https://positivepsychology.com/benefits-
    of-meditation.

Choose the Glass Half Full

"a positive attitude improves your health": Jane Framingham, "Positive Thinking Improves Physical Health," PsychCentral, January 14, 2020, https://psychcentral.com/lib/the-power-of-positive-thinking.

"a positive mindset at work": "Positive Thinking in the Workplace," Indeed, December 12, 2019, https://www.indeed.com/career-advice/career-development/positive-thinking-in-your-career.

"Sally was at the peak . . . six successful novels to date": Sally Koslow, interview with the author, April 7, 2020.

"I followed every Rx for landing a job . . . magazine": Sally Koslow, "Sally Koslow: Lessons Learned from a Midlife Pink Slip," *Psychology Today*, June 13, 2013, https://www.psychologytoday.com/us/blog/one-true-thing/201306/sally-koslow-lessons-learned-midlife-pink-slip.

"Would employers start to think . . . girls club": Koslow, "Lessons Learned from a Midlife Pink Slip."

Hang with Your Girlfriends

"mutuality matters": Kare Anderson, *Mutuality Matters: How You Can Create More Opportunity, Adventure, and Friendship with Others* (self-published, 2017).

"studies demonstrate the benefits of friendship": Suwen Lin, Louis Faust, Pablo Robles-Granda, Tomasz Kajdanowicz, and Nitesh Chawla, "Social Network Structure Is Predictive of Health and Wellness," Plos One, June 6, 2019, https://journals.plos.org/plosone/article?id=10.1371/journal.pone.0217264.

"Some recommend that you hang with your girlfriends twice a week": Melissa Locker, "Women Should Go Out with Their Girlfriends Twice a Week, According to Research," *Southern Living*, July 10, 2020, https://www.southernliving.com/healthy-living/spending-time-with-friends-good-for-you.

"Women more reliably . . . mortality": Shelley E. Taylor, "Tend and Befriend Theory," accessed July 10, 2020, https://taylorlab.psych.ucla.edu/wp-content/uploads/sites/5/2014/11/2011_Tend-and-Befriend-Theory.pdf.

"Socializing with friends helps older women": Archana Singh and Nishi Misra, "Loneliness, Depression and Sociability in Old Age," *Industrial Psychology Journal* 18, no. 1 (January–June 2009): 51–55, doi:10.4103/0972-6748.57861; Andrea Brandt, "Are Female Friendships the Key to Happiness in

Older Women?" *Psychology Today*, February 26, 2018, https://www.psycho
logytoday.com/us/blog/mindful-anger/201802/are-female-friendships-the-
key-happiness-in-older-women.

"When Dale Pollekoff moved to Los Angeles . . . 2,700 members": Rosette Rago,
"Finding Female Friends Over 50 Can Be Hard. These Women Figured It
Out," *New York Times*, December 31, 2018, https://www.nytimes.com/2018
/12/31/style/self-care/finding-female-friends-over-50-meetup.html.

Move from Sadass to Badass

"Words are singularly . . . to humiliate, and to humble": Yehuda Berg quoted in
Marci Marra, "The Power of Your Words," Thrive Global, October 15, 2019,
https://thriveglobal.com/stories/the-power-of-your-words-2.

About the Author

AWARD-WINNING ENTREPRENEUR, *Forbes* contributing writer, and executive coach Bonnie Marcus, MEd, assists professional women in successfully navigating the workplace and positioning and promoting themselves to advance their careers.

With twenty-plus years of sales and management experience, Bonnie's extensive business background includes CEO of a ServiceMaster company and VP of sales at Medical Staffing Network and two other national companies in the health care and software industries. She has held executive positions in start-ups and Fortune 500 companies.

Bonnie started her corporate career at an entry-level position and worked her way up to the top of a national company. Her passion is now to help other women embrace their talent and ambition, to step into their full potential and workplace power.

Bonnie shares her message globally through speaking engagements, live and virtual workshops, blogging, and her popular podcast, *Badass Women at Any Age*.

In addition to *Forbes*, Bonnie has been published in the *Chicago Tribune*, *Fast Company*, *Entrepreneur*, *Business Insider*, Daily Worth, Women of HR, Fairygodboss, *Forge Medium*, and on HR.com. She has also been featured by the *Wall Street Journal*, BBC *Business Daily*,

LA Times, Huffington Post, Fortune, Reader's Digest, Diversity MBA, Dow Jones Moneyish, *Levo League, Upstart Business Journal, Psychology Today*, Crains NY Business, *Men's Health*, and CIO *Magazine*, among others.

A certified coach, Bonnie has been honored by Global Gurus as one of the world's top thirty coaches from 2015 to 2020. She has been acknowledged as one of the top 100 keynote speakers in 2018 by Databird Research Journal.

Bonnie received a BA from Connecticut College and an MEd from New York University.

Bonnie's website is www.BonnieMarcusLeadership.com. She can be reached by email at Bonnie@BonnieMarcusLeadership.com and on Twitter @selfpromote and Instagram @self_promote_. Read her articles on *Forbes* at www.forbes.com/sites/bonniemarcus. Her podcast is available on Apple Podcasts.